Flavours of Piedmont

Flavours of Italy

MARIAPAOLA DÈTTORE
GABRIELLA GANUGI

PIEDMONT

NH
NEW
HOLLAND

First published in 1999 by
New Holland Publishers (UK) Ltd
London • Cape Town • Sydney • Auckland

24 Nutford Place
London W1H 6DQ
United Kingdom

Level 1, Unit 4, 14 Aquatic Drive
Frenchs Forest, NSW 2086
Australia

80 McKenzie Street
Cape Town 8001
South Africa

Unit 1A, 218 Lake Road
Northcote, Auckland
New Zealand

ISBN 1 85974 188 6

This book was conceived, edited, and designed by
McRae Books Srl, Florence, Italy.

Text: Mariapaola Dèttore and Gabriella Ganugi
Photography: Marco Lanza
Set Design: Rosalba Gioffrè
Design: Marco Nardi
Translation from the Italian: First Edition
Editing: Alison Leach, Anne McRae
Layout and cutouts: Ornella Fassio, Adriano Nardi

2 4 6 8 10 9 7 5 3 1

Colour separations: Fotolito Toscana, Florence, Italy
Printed and bound in Italy by Grafiche Editoriale Padane

Contents

Introduction

Piedmont, from the Latin *Pede montis* (foot hills), lies at the foot of the European Alps in northwestern Italy. It is the largest region on the Italian mainland. To the north, stretching toward the Alps and France, lies the tiny region of Val d'Aosta. The culinary habits and traditions in this long, upland valley are very similar to those in Piedmont, so we will consider the two together in this book. Piedmont is one of Italy's most diverse regions, with mountains, foothills, and plains producing a wide range of produce for a rich and varied cuisine.

Toward the end of the nineteenth century, the bourgeoisie became the new rising class in Italy and, with the gradual disappearance of cooks from private households, the role of the housewife was redefined. The Italian edition of Louis Eustache Audot's *The Town and Country Cook or New Economical Cookery*, translated from the original French text and published in Turin in 1845, represents one of the first attempts to provide housewives with recipes, information, and advice. Audot describes a practical and simple way of cooking, very different from the recipe books of Napoleonic France which reflected that era's obsession with grandeur.

At the end of his book, Audot states that in his experience, most of the dishes served in Italian households were of French origin, adapted to suit local tastes and bearing little resemblance to the original. The influence of French cuisine on Piedmontese cookery is undisguised, and is due to geographical proximity and the fact that Piedmont was once part of the Kingdom of Savoy, an area encompassing northwest Italy and southeast France. French was spoken until the mid-nineteenth century, and French cooking was considered to be the most refined. It was adopted by aristocratic families not only in Piedmont but

Piedmont was the leading state in the Risorgimento, the ideological and literary movement that brought independence and unity to Italy. Camillo Benso, better known under his Piedmontese title of Count Cavour, and Giuseppe Garibaldi were the most prominent figures in this movement. When the Kingdom of Italy was finally established in 1861, the King of Piedmont, Victor Emmanuel II (above), became the first king of the modern state while Cavour was elected as the first Prime Minister.

Left: Café Baratti e Milano, in Piazza Castello, Turin.

A rustic Piedmontese culinary tradition exists in the upland areas of Langhe and Monferrato. These areas' well-loved landscapes have been immortalized by many of Italy's greatest writers; Cesare Pavese, Beppe Fenoglio, and Giovanni Arpino have all eloquently described the beauty of the Langhe hills, extolling the charms of the picturesque countryside where the broad horizons are punctuated with towers and castles and sharply pointed hilltops. These areas now provide some of the best gastronomic itineraries for tourists in search of fine wines and outstanding food.

throughout Italy. The local dialect spoken today remains a mixture of Italian and French, while nearly all Piedmontese cookery terms are French.

In common with other regions of Italy, Piedmont has historically possessed two parallel culinary traditions: one, refined and exclusive for the wealthy classes and another, far humbler, relying on the use of leftovers and seasonal foods bought cheaply in local markets. The latter offered a varied and nutritious diet which, without losing touch with its simple peasant origins, gradually developed more subtlety and originality.

To this day, elaborate and refined dishes, created by great French chefs of the past, coexist with time-honored, simple flavors, created by people who ate to live but transformed this necessity into an art, however modest. These twin traditions have given rise to a rich and varied cuisine that can boast the widest range of hot and cold appetizers in Italy, including the delicately flavored, truffle-scented cured meats known as *Carne all'Albese,* as well as full-flavored, sustaining pasta dishes, such as *Agnolotti* (see recipe, page 46) served with wafer-thin truffle slices and butter. Main courses include the celebrated mixed boiled meats known as *Baié* (see recipe, page 64) served with *Bagnet Verd* (see recipe, page 15) or *Bagnet Ross* (see recipe, page 16); braised meat dishes, the most famous of which is made with Barolo wine (see recipe, page 69), another of Piedmont's culinary glories; *Vitello Tonnato* (see recipe, page 71) for which cooked veal is carved into very thin slices and served with tuna and caper mayonnaise; brook trout and other freshwater fish. Then come Piedmont's cheeses, such as fontina and robiola and, lastly, some of the most famous Italian desserts: *Panna Cotta* (see recipe, page 102), which is cream cooked with sugar and vanilla, then poured into molds and chilled (these custard creams are served with a chocolate or fruit sauce); *Zabaione,* a frothy confection of eggs, sugar, and Marsala wine (see recipe, page 103), and *Mont Blanc* (see recipe, page 101), puréed sweet chestnuts with whipped cream.

It is difficult to place the most distinctive Piedmontese recipe *Bagna Cauda* (see recipe, page 24) within a specific course. It has such a wealth of ingredients that it can be considered a meal in itself. In Piedmont it is seen as the perfect expression of conviviality, served when a crowd of family or friends are gathered around the table to enjoy good conversation while dipping vegetables in the savory sauce made with anchovies, butter, olive oil, and garlic. Some versions include the addition of cream or other ingredients to tone down the flavor, with questionable results. *Bagna Cauda* is a robust dish, with a strong, uncompromising taste, best consumed on freezing cold winter days. It is served very hot (in keeping with its Italian name which, translated literally, means "hot bath"), in a deep earthenware dish placed over a little spirit stove in the center of the table. The prepared vegetables are dipped directly into it. The recipe for *Bagna Cauda* varies slightly from valley to valley: in Nizza Monferrato and throughout the Belbo Valley it is customary to chop the garlic very finely after soaking it in milk to lessen the intensity of its odor and make it more digestible. Some Monferrato cooks add half a glass of Barbera wine after dissolving the anchovies in the oil. In Alba, the garlic is crushed, while in the Pinerolo area most of the vegetables used for dipping are boiled or baked in the oven.

Butter is used in many Piedmontese dishes, in common with virtually the whole of northern Italy where it is used in preference to olive oil as a cooking fat because of its more delicate taste, which attenuates the robust flavors of some dishes and emphasizes the subtlety of others.

The province of Alba is famous for its legendary white truffles, the most highly prized in Europe. Apart from their size, it is their scent which makes them so sought-after. With their dogs to guide them in their patient and determined search for this precious fungus, the *trifulau* or "truffle hunters" are mysterious, taciturn characters, unearthing the biggest truffles to exhibit at

Wines are an integral part of the local culinary tradition and it is impossible to savor a Piedmontese meal without the help of the strong, full-bodied wines which go so well with the oldest, most traditional dishes. The celebrated red (Barbera, Barbaresco, Barolo, and Gattinara) and sparkling wines are now being joined by several excellent whites. Most Barbera is produced in the Asti area; it goes well with meat dishes, especially roasts, as does Barolo, which is produced in the Langhe. Gattinara, from the Vercelli district, is made from the Nebbiolo grape which takes its name from nebbia, *the fog which envelops the vines in late October when the grapes are ripe for picking.*

MEDITERRANEAN SEA

local fairs and markets. The truffles are eaten raw, shaved into wafer-thin slices, usually with simple dishes, adding their incomparable flavor and aroma to eggs, cheese fondue, and *Tajarin* (the local version of tagliatelle). One of the greatest truffle enthusiasts was Gioacchino Rossini, a very discerning gourmet besides being a great composer, and *Oeufs en Chemise alla Rossini* has become part of the repertoire of haute cuisine. But Alba is not only famous for its truffles; it is also the home town of the confectionery manufacturer, Ferrero, producer of some irresistible modern delicacies such as Nutella, the hazelnut and chocolate spread, and Rochers, sophisticated hazelnut chocolates.

Meat is the main ingredient of the most traditional Piedmontese dishes: the *Baié* (see recipe, page 64), proudly served on special occasions, is of peasant origin and calls for many types of meat: tongue, little sausages, beef cuts, pork skin, calf's head, pig's feet (trotters), chicken, capon, and veal, as well as a wide variety of vegetables. Its preparation is a rite in the Piedmontese kitchen.

The Piedmontese show little enthusiasm for spaghetti as a first course, but they adore risotto (rice is produced in abundance on the plains of Vercelli), and clear, broth-based soups. Among the most remarkable risottos, the version made with Alba truffles occupies a place of honor, as do the Frogs' Legs Risotto from the area between Vercelli and Novara, and the classic *Risotto al Barolo*, made with equal quantities of stock and red wine. *Paniscia* is a typical local soup, with rice cooked in vegetable stock, to which a tender, cooked sausage and cheese are added.

Piedmontese *Fritto Misto* (Mixed Fried Meats) differs from similar dishes in other regions of Italy for the mixture of beaten egg, flour, and breadcrumbs used to coat the ingredients (lamb cutlets, brains, liver, and more) which make up the mixed fry. Small, sweet, semolina croquettes are served with the fried meats throughout the region, while local preference determines whether other, less typical ingredients, such as amaretti cookies, or sausage meat rissoles are added.

The entrance to local government offices in the provincial town of Alessandria. The rhythms of life in the smaller centers are calm and "human-friendly."

An old farmhouse with typical Piedmontese architecture is surrounded by rice paddies near Vercelli.

Turin is Piedmont's only real city; the others are more provincial and relaxed, with atmospheres more akin to those of large country towns than bustling urban centers.

A palio (horse race), dating back to 1275, and preceded by an historic procession, is held in Asti on the second Sunday in September. There is a strange prize for the competitor who comes last: an anchovy!

Piedmont has few rivals elsewhere in Italy when it comes to desserts, cakes, and confectionery: many of these were created by French cooks at the royal court of Savoy, and have since become internationally famous.

Turin is not only the capital of Piedmont; it was here that chocolate was first manufactured in Europe. At the end of the sixteenth century, Duke Emanuel Philibert of Savoy brought some cocoa home from Spain and the first chocolate-making experiments took place in this city. By the end of the eighteenth century it had become the international capital of chocolate. Gianduiotti chocolates, named after Gianduja, a local legendary character, are the most typical of its world-famous products.

The city of Turin underwent its greatest transformation during the end of the nineteenth and the beginning of the twentieth century, when it changed from being the capital of the Kingdom of Savoy to being first the hometown of the Italian movie industry and then the capital of Italian mass automobile manufacturing. In the early twentieth century the first studios and the factory of a company called *Fabbrica Italiana Automobili Torino* (Fiat) both started production. The latter subsequently became part of the country's economic boom with its dream of a motorcar for everyone. Turin is an elegant city, with its bridges over the River Po and baroque architecture, but it does not possess a distinctive cuisine of its own which differs from the rest of the region's cooking. The foodstuff most closely identified with this city (apart from the Gianduiotto chocolates made with butter, cocoa, and hazelnuts) are probably Grissini, very thin, crisp sticks of bread. The French Emperor Napoleon was passionately fond of these and had great quantities of "*les petits batons de Turin*" sent to him.

Asti is a quiet and reserved town of towers and churches, despite being the center of the Italian *spumante* (sparkling wine) industry. Founded by the Romans, the city later formed part of the dowry which Giangaleazzo Visconti bestowed on his daughter Valentina when she married the French Prince Louis d'Orleans. *Fricandû* is a specialty of the Asti district; this stew is made with mixed cuts of beef and garlic, vinegar, baby onions, rosemary, and pork fat.

Alessandria is an important agricultural center situated beside the River Tanaro. It was named after Pope Alexander III. Napoleon's victory on the battlefield of Marengo is rivaled in fame by a local dessert of the same name, made with whipped cream.

Originally a Celtic-Ligurian settlement, the town of **Vercelli** enjoyed its moment of splendor in the early thirteenth century. Typical dishes from this area are *Lepre in Vivet*, hare marinated in red wine and cooked with aromatic herbs (jugged hare). Saragnon is a local cheese made with leftover curds from gorgonzola production and fragments of fermented cheeses, which are then mixed with alcohol and left to ferment for a month until creamy, full-flavored, and very strong.

Cuneo takes it name ("wedge") from the way the houses and street plan follow the contours of a high, flat, wedge-shaped site jutting out between two rivers. It is famous for large, rum chocolates called *Cuneesi* and for *Brus*, a cheese made with a mixture of other cheeses which are left to ferment and then fortified with grappa; it is so strong that it can be eaten only in very small quantities! *Gnocchi alla Bava*, potato dumplings tossed in butter, cream, and melted fontina cheese are typical of Cuneo's cooking. Within the province of Cuneo, Govone is renowned for its *Zampone* (Stuffed Pig's Foot/Trotter).

Novara is famous for two types of cured goose meat. The stronger tasting one is raw and hung for several days to dry cure. The other is first simmered in water for about 1 hour; then dry cured in a cool place. It has a more delicate, subtle flavor. Formerly, when pigs were butchered, *Marzapani* or *Sanguinacci* (blood puddings) were made by soaking bread in the pig's blood and adding pieces of pork fat. These were then boiled and sliced.

Sunset over the paddy fields of Piedmont: sixty percent of the rice consumed in Italy is produced on the plain which stretches between Novara and Vercelli.

Piazza Galimberti in Cuneo with its magnificent backdrop of the Maritime Alps. The second town in the province is Alba, famous for its truffles.

Salse e Santipasti

If the idea of sampling up to ten or twelve tempting and tiny helpings of tidbits before you start the main part of your meal is appealing, Piedmont is definitely the region for you. The main danger is overindulging at the beginning of the meal and being unable to appreciate later courses. To start this chapter we have included four basic sauces, which will be of use throughout the book. *Bagna Cauda* (Hot Piedmontese Dip) is the most distinctive among the many appetizers from this region, while the *Fondue* made with tasty alpine fontina cheese is probably the most famous.

Bagnet Verd

Green Sauce

Soak the breadcrumbs for a few minutes in the vinegar (diluted with a little cold water if it is very strong) and then squeeze out excess moisture. ❧ Place the egg yolk in a bowl and mash with a fork. Add the parsley, garlic, anchovy, and breadcrumbs and mix well. ❧ Trickle in sufficient oil to make a fairly thick sauce while stirring continuously. Season to taste with salt (if using anchovies, the sauce may already be salty enough) and freshly ground white pepper. ❧ The sauce can also be made in a blender. In that case, place all the ingredients in the blender (the parsley and garlic will not need to be chopped), and process for 2–3 minutes. ❧ Leave to stand for at least 30 minutes, preferably 1 hour, before serving. Stir carefully and serve.

Serves 4

Preparation: 15–20 minutes + at least 30 minutes' standing

Recipe grading: easy

- ¹⁄₂ cup/1 oz/30 g fresh white breadcrumbs
- 3–4 tablespoons red wine vinegar
- 1 hard-cooked /hard-boiled egg yolk
- 3 tablespoons finely chopped parsley
- 1–2 cloves garlic, finely chopped
- 1 salted anchovy, rinsed and boned, or 2–3 anchovy fillets (optional)
- scant ¹⁄₂ cup/3¹⁄₂ fl oz/100 ml extra-virgin olive oil
- salt to taste
- freshly ground white pepper

This sauce, together with Bagnet Ross *(Warm Red Sauce, see recipe, page 16) is served with* Baié *(Mixed Boiled Meats). It is also very good when served with boiled or steamed fish. If serving with fish, omit the vinegar and use the same quantity of freshly squeezed lemon juice. For a more pungent sauce, add one or more of the following ingredients (finely chopped):1–2 teaspoons capers; 1 gherkin; a slice of raw onion or 2 pickled pearl onions.*

Bagnet Ross
Warm Red Sauce

Serves 4
Preparation: 25 minutes
Cooking: 1½ hours
Recipe grading: easy

- 1¼ lb/625 g ripe tomatoes
- 1 small onion, coarsely chopped
- 1 tender stalk celery (with leaves), coarsely chopped
- 1 small carrot, coarsely chopped
- 1 clove garlic, finely chopped
- 2 teaspoons finely chopped parsley
- 1 chile pepper
- 3–4 tablespoons extra-virgin olive oil
- 1 teaspoon Dijon-type mustard
- 1 tablespoon red wine vinegar
- salt to taste

Blanch the tomatoes for 1 minute in boiling water, then peel. Cut in half and remove the seeds. Set aside to drain for 15 minutes in a colander, cut side downward. ❧ Prepare the other vegetables while the tomatoes are draining. ❧ Cut the tomatoes into small pieces and place them in a saucepan with the other vegetables, garlic, and parsley. Add the chile pepper and cook over a low heat, uncovered, for 1½ hours, stirring frequently. ❧ Sieve the contents of the saucepan (or reduce them to a purée in a food processor), then blend in the oil, mustard, and vinegar. Add salt to taste and serve hot. ❧ This sauce can be prepared in advance and reheated just before serving. Stored in an airtight container, it will keep well in the refrigerator for several days. ❧ To give the sauce an agreeable sweet-sour taste, add more vinegar (scant ½ cup/3½ fl oz/100 ml) and 1 tablespoon sugar after the other ingredients have cooked for 1 hour. ❧ Use more or less chile pepper depending on how hot you like your sauce.

This sauce is often served, together with Bagnet Verd *(Green Sauce, see recipe, page 15) with the splendid selection of boiled meats in Piedmont's traditional* Baié *(Mixed Boiled Meats, see recipe, page 64).*

Salsa del Povr'om

Poor Man's Sauce

Serves 4
Preparation: 2–3 minutes
Cooking: 7–9 minutes
Recipe grading: easy

- 3 tablespoons/1½ oz/45g butter
- 1–2 whole cloves garlic, peeled and lightly crushed
- 1 teaspoon all-purpose/plain flour
- 2 tablespoons red wine vinegar
- salt to taste
- freshly ground white pepper
- 2 whole eggs + 1 extra yolk

Melt the butter in a small saucepan over a low heat. Add the garlic cloves and cook very slowly until they turn a pale golden color (if browned they will give the sauce a bitter flavor). ➷ Mix the flour into the vinegar in a bowl and season with salt and pepper to taste. Add the whole eggs and the extra yolk and beat very lightly with a fork, making sure they don't become frothy. ➷ Remove the garlic from the butter and add the egg mixture gradually while stirring continuously over a very low heat. Continue stirring until the mixture thickens to a smooth, creamy consistency. ➷ Serve warm or at room temperature.

This sauce goes very well with cooked vegetables (snow peas/mange-tout, French beans, asparagus) tossed in butter, and with boiled or roast meat and poultry and veal escalopes.
A much older, eponymous sauce, no longer used in Italy, was very like the English recipe for Poor Man's Sauce, made with shallots or onion, pickled vegetables, and parsley, and served with boiled meats. The modern version, given here, is completely different.

Saussa d'Avije

Honey Sauce

Serves 4
Preparation: 20 minutes
Recipe grading: easy

Pound the walnuts finely using a mortar and pestle, or grind in a food processor. ❧ Mix the honey and mustard in a small bowl. Add the stock or water and then the walnuts. Stir thoroughly. ❧ Serve warm or at room temperature.

- 12 peeled walnut halves
- scant ¾ cup/5–6 fl oz/150–180 ml mild, liquid honey
- 2 tablespoons mustard
- 1–2 tablespoons hot stock (homemade or bouillon cube) or water

This sauce is served with boiled or roast meats and keeps well in a sealed jar in the refrigerator for several days. In Piedmontese dialect it is known as "bees' sauce" since they provide the honey for it.

Fondua

Fontina Cheese Fondue

Serves 4

*Preparation: 10 minutes + 2–4 hours'
    standing*

Cooking: 10 minutes

Recipe grading: fairly easy

- 14 oz/400 g (net weight without rind),
  fontina valdostana cheese
- 1 cup/8 fl oz/250 ml whole milk
- 2 tablespoons/1 oz/30g butter
- 4–5 egg yolks
- salt to taste
- freshly ground white pepper
- slices of toast

*Suggested wine: a dry red
    (Nebbiolo d'Alba)*

Slice the cheese thinly and place in a bowl with enough milk to cover. Leave to stand for 2–4 hours. ❧ Half-fill a saucepan or the bottom pan of a double boiler with water and bring to a very gentle boil. Place a heatproof bowl or the top pan of the double boiler containing the butter over it then leave to melt. ❧ Drain the milk off from the cheese, reserving the milk. Add the cheese to the melted butter, together with 3–4 tablespoons of the reserved milk. ❧ Stir continuously with a balloon whisk or wooden spoon over the gently simmering water until the cheese has melted and threads start to form. At no point during preparation should it be allowed to boil. ❧ Adding one at a time, stir the first 4 egg yolks into the cheese, incorporating each of them very thoroughly. The mixture should now be glossy and smooth. If it still looks a little grainy, add the final, fifth egg yolk and stir well for 1 minute. ❧ Season with salt and white pepper to taste. ❧ Transfer the fondue into 4 very hot, shallow, earthenware bowls. Serve with thickly sliced toasted French bread. ❧ The gourmet version of this fondue is served with a sprinkling of wafer-thin slices of white truffles from the Alba region.

Fondue is one of the glories of Piedmontese cooking and deservedly famous. Although closely related to Swiss fondue, its preparation and taste differ noticeably. With the best fontina cheese and careful cooking, this recipe should not present any problems. However, if it does curdle or separate, mix scant 1 tablespoon cornstarch (cornflour) with 2 tablespoons of the reserved, cold milk, then stir it quickly into the fondue, which will become smooth and homogenous. This fondue can also be used as a sauce for Piedmontese Risotto *(see recipe, page 44), as well as for plain boiled rice, tagliatelle, polenta, and agnolotti. In the Val d'Aosta it is served as a topping for slices of bread fried in butter.*

Cheese Fondue: an Alpine Specialty

Fondue is made in all the alpine valleys of the European Alps, but the fondue of Val d'Aosta is considered the most classic of them all. A simple mixture of fontina cheese, butter, egg yolk, and milk, it is cooked over a low heat so that the mixture never boils. The many different versions of fondue are, along with *Bagna Cauda*, among the oldest and most traditional dishes in Piedmontese and Val d'Aosta cuisine. The basic ingredients: cheese, milk, polenta, and bread, lie at the very heart of these culinary traditions.

Like many other regional recipes, fondue is not a sophisticated dish, but meant to be shared by close friends and family gathered around a fondue pot before a blazing fire on cold winter evenings. The sharing of bread and polenta, dipped into the common pot, brings back the intimacy of days gone by. The cheese-based dish is high in energy and protein, just right to revive body and soul after a hard day's work in the mountain air and, more recently, after a long day's skiing on the slopes.

Fondue made in the area around Alba is ennobled by the addition to the hot cheese mixture of wafer-thin slices of the local white truffles. In some parts of Piedmont, fontina cheese is replaced by an ancient local cheese called bra, from the town of the same name. Fondue from Valcamonica is made with casolet cheese and served with pieces of roasted dice of polenta for dipping.

Fondue is best served with the classic red wines typical of the regions: dry, with plenty of body, such as Barbera d'Asti, which mingles in the mouth with the cheese, exalting its personality to the full.

Bagna Cauda
Hot Piedmontese Dip

Serves 4
Preparation: 10 minutes
Cooking: about 1 hour
Recipe grading: easy

- 6 tablespoons/3 oz/80 g sweet/ unsalted butter
- 6 cloves garlic, very finely chopped
- 1 cup/8 fl oz/250 ml extra-virgin olive oil
- 4 oz/125 g anchovy fillets
- selection of fresh, raw vegetables, including: cardoon stalks (peeled and kept in cold water acidulated with lemon juice until just before serving to prevent discoloration); celery stalks; tender Savoy cabbage leaves; cauliflower florets; sliced baby turnips; carrots (sometimes boiled until just tender); peeled, sliced Jerusalem artichokes; radishes; raw or roast sweet bell peppers/capsicums

Suggested wine: a young, dry red (Barbera d'Asti)

Melt the butter in a small fireproof earthenware casserole or saucepan. Add the garlic and cook over a very gentle heat for 15 minutes. The garlic should not take on any color. ❧ Add the oil and leave over a very low heat for 10 minutes more. ❧ Add the anchovy fillets and cook as gently as possible for 30–40 minutes. Stir frequently with a wooden spoon and use the back of it to mash the anchovies, which should gradually dissolve into the oil and butter. The sauce should never reach boiling point. ❧ There are a number of delicious variations on the basic recipe. Try adding a scant $\frac{1}{2}$ cup/$3\frac{1}{2}$ fl oz/ 100 ml heavy (double) cream 5 minutes before the end of cooking time for a very rich sauce. ❧ Add wafer-thin slices of fresh truffle just before serving. ❧ Crumble 3–4 walnut halves together with the oil to recreate the traditional flavor of walnut oil.

In the days when walnut oil was widely available, it was used in place of the olive oil. Traditionally, Bagna Cauda is made in a small fireproof earthenware pot which is placed in the center of the table and kept hot over a spirit lamp (formerly a small brazier containing embers). This means that everyone seated round the table can easily reach over to dip the prepared raw vegetables into the sauce. The vegetables should be arranged on a large serving platter.

Insalata di Carne Cruda
Raw Veal Salad

Serves 4
Preparation: 10 minutes
Recipe grading: easy

- 4 cups/1 lb/500 g ground lean, tender veal
- 6 tablespoons extra-virgin olive oil
- ⅓ clove garlic, very finely chopped
- 4–5 tablespoons freshly squeezed lemon juice
- 2 tablespoons cold water
- salt to taste
- freshly ground white pepper

Suggested wine: a dry red (Freisa d'Asti)

Place the meat in a mixing bowl and gradually add all the other ingredients, mixing very thoroughly and tasting at intervals to decide whether there is enough lemon juice. ❧ There are two schools of thought concerning this mouthwatering salad: one maintains that the meat should be served immediately after preparation, the other that the meat should be left in a cold place for a few hours to allow time for the flavors to develop and for the meat to be "cooked" by the lemon juice. Compromise by preparing it 30 minutes before serving and it will still be an attractive rosy color. ❧ Lift and turn the mixture with a fork at the last minute to make it lighter and less compact. ❧ Serve with slivers of truffle or sliced raw mushrooms.

To achieve the best texture for this excellent salad, chop 1 lb/500 g trimmed veal tenderloin (fillet or noix) finely with a very sharp knife. This requires a little patience and preparation will take longer than the time given above.

Insalata di Riso
Rice Salad

Cook the rice in plenty of boiling salted water until tender but still slightly firm to the bite. ❧ Drain in a colander and rinse briefly under cold running water to stop the cooking process and to prevent the grains sticking together. Drain thoroughly and transfer to a salad bowl. ❧ Pour the oil and lemon juice into a large mixing bowl. Add the egg yolk and use a fork to crush it into the oil and lemon juice. ❧ Add the anchovy then mix to make a well-blended dressing. ❧ Add the tuna, capers, and olives, and season with salt and pepper. ❧ Pour this dressing over the rice and mix gently but thoroughly. Garnish with pickled vegetables, if liked.

Serves 4
Preparation: 15 minutes
Cooking: 13–15 minutes
Recipe grading: easy

- 1½ cups/10 oz/300 g Italian Arborio rice
- 5 tablespoons extra-virgin olive oil
- 2 tablespoons lemon juice
- 1 hard-cooked (hard-boiled) egg yolk
- 2 anchovy fillets, finely chopped
- a 7 oz/200 g can of tuna in olive oil, flaked
- 1 tablespoon capers
- 10–12 pitted mild green olives in brine, thinly sliced
- salt to taste
- freshly ground white pepper
- pickled vegetables to garnish (optional)

Suggested wine: a dry, fruity red
(Nebbiolo d'Alba)

Insalata Capricciosa

Mixed Ham and Tongue Salad

Serves 4
Preparation: 20 minutes
Recipe grading: easy

Slice the ham and tongue into julienne strips. ❧ Slice the mushrooms thinly. ❧ Peel the celeriac and cut into julienne strips, sprinkling with lemon juice to prevent discoloration. ❧ Place these four ingredients in a large bowl and mix with the mayonnaise. ❧ Transfer to a serving dish and garnish, if liked, with a selection of pickled vegetables.

- 4 oz/125 g lean cooked ham
- 4 oz/125 g cooked pickled ox tongue
- ½ cup/3 oz/90 g mushrooms preserved in oil
- 1 large celery root (celeriac) —
- juice of ½ lemon
- ¾-1 cup/6–8 fl oz/180–250 ml mayonnaise (preferably homemade with 1 egg yolk; scant ½ cup/3½ fl oz/ 100 ml extra-virgin olive oil; lemon juice; salt; pepper)
- pickled vegetables for garnish (optional)

Suggested wine: a young, dry red (Barbera d'Asti)

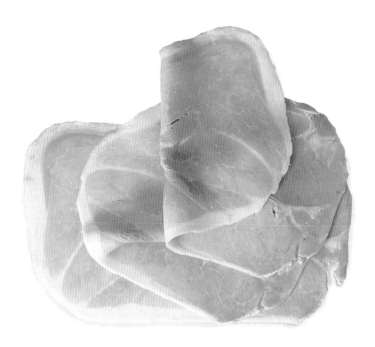

Salads play an important role in the gastronomy of Piedmont: this is one of the most typical recipes.

Trota in Carpione
Marinated Trout

Serves 4

Preparation: 20 minutes + 24 hours' standing

Cooking: 10–15 minutes

Recipe grading: easy

- 4 small trout, each weighing around 12 oz/350 g (or 12–16 small trout fillets)
- 6 tablespoons/3 oz/90 g butter
- 5 fresh sage leaves
- small sprig fresh thyme

FOR THE MARINADE:
- ²/₃ cup/5 fl oz/150 ml white wine vinegar
- ²/₃ cup/5 fl oz/150 ml dry white wine
- 1–2 bay leaves
- 6 lightly crushed juniper berries
- 15 fresh sage leaves
- 1 large onion, sliced about ¹/₈ in/3–4 mm thick
- ¹/₂ teaspoon salt

Suggested wine: a very dry white (Cortese di Gavi)

This recipe is also used for other freshwater fish (fillets of tench, carp, barbel), as well as for very small, whole fish which need much shorter cooking times.

Trim and draw (gut) the fish. Rinse well inside and out, then dry with paper towels. ✎ Place the butter, sage leaves, and thyme in a wide skillet (frying pan) over a fairly high heat. The butter will foam gently as it heats; as soon as this foam has subsided, it is hot enough to add the trout. ✎ After the trout have fried for about 5 minutes on one side, turn them over and fry for another 5 minutes, or until they are done. ✎ While the fish are cooking, make the marinade. Bring the vinegar and wine to a boil with the bay leaves, juniper berries, sage leaves, onion, and salt in a saucepan. Leave to simmer over a moderate heat for 3–4 minutes. Turn off the heat. ✎ As soon as the trout are done, transfer to a fairly deep dish just large enough to contain them in a single layer. Sprinkle with the hot marinade and its flavorings. Leave to cool at room temperature. ✎ When cold, cover the dish with a piece of plastic wrap (cling film) or foil. Leave in a cool place (not in the refrigerator) for at least 24 hours before serving. ✎ Prepared in this way, marinated fish will keep for 5–6 days.

The Heartlands of Piedmont

Langhe and Monferrato cover the rolling hills that extend from the town of Casale Monferrato to the Ligurian Appennines. The beautiful landscape, and the history and traditions of these hills are quintessentially Piedmontese. The word "langa" means the crest of a hill, while Monferrato takes its name from an aristocratic family that ruled here during the Middle Ages. The everchanging and

often harsh landscape in the Langhe has been celebrated by its famous sons, particularly the anti-facist writer, editor, and translator, Cesare Pavese. These are the most often visited areas of Piedmont, where the food and wine combine with the warmth of character of the local inhabitants, the treasures of art and history, and the beauty of the landscape, to make any visit unforgettable.

Alba, the city of the hundred towers, is the largest in the Langhe. A well-known gastronomical center, every year it holds the Fiera del tartufo *(Truffles fair) when the season's best truffle is chosen. Alba is not only famous for its truffles and wine, but also for its cheese and chocolates. The Ferrero chocolate factory is here, exporting its products all over the world. The cafés in the town are well worth a visit for their exquisite Barolo- and rum-filled chocolates, hazelnut cake, and* Mont Blanc *(see recipe, page 101).*

Ninety percent of Piedmont's extraordinary wine (see The Red Wines of Piedmont, pages 72–73) is produced in the Monferrato hills around Asti and Alessandria and in the Langhe around Alba and Canelli. The areas' proverbial mists, which linger in the valleys in the early autumn when the hot summer months are over, allow the grapes to ripen slowly on the vines.

A highly prized local variety of hazelnut is widely cultivated in the Langhe. Recently granted official certification of origin, it is used in many of the local confectionery products. Every year, at the end of August, a festival in honor of the hazelnut and the regional specialty Torta di Nocciole (Hazelnut Cake) takes place in Cortemilia.

The city of Asti – famous throughout the world for its sparkling white spumante wines – lies at the center of the rolling hills of the Monferrato area. The countryside round about is dotted with castles and every small town or village has at least one. The celebrated Italian poet Giosuè Carducci, winner of the Nobel Prize for Literature in 1906, described these hills as "throbbing with castles and vineyards."

Peperoni all'Acciuga
Roasted Bell Peppers with Anchovy Dressing

Serves 4

Preparation: 25 minutes + 1 hour's resting

Cooking: 25 minutes

Recipe grading: easy

- 2–3 medium yellow or red bell peppers/capsicums
- salt to taste
- 2–3 cloves garlic, thinly sliced
- 4–6 tablespoons extra-virgin olive oil
- 8–10 anchovy fillets

Suggested wine: a very dry white (Cortese di Gavi)

The rich, sweet flavor of the bell peppers is even better if they are roasted over a charcoal-fired grill or directly over the burner of a gas stove. Covered with plastic wrap (cling film) or foil, this dish will keep well in the refrigerator for several days. Take the bell peppers out of the refrigerator a few hours before serving, so that they are at room temperature.

To roast the bell peppers, place them whole under the broiler (grill) under a fairly high heat, giving them quarter turns as their skin scorches and blackens. The whole process will take about 20 minutes, by which time the peppers will have released a lot of moisture and become floppy. Wrap them in foil (not too tightly) without delay. Leave for 10 minutes before unwrapping and the skin will peel away easily. ✌ Cut the bell peppers in half from top to bottom and discard the stalks, seeds, and the pulpy inner core. Rinse under cold running water to get rid of any remaining burnt bits. ✌ Slice the bell peppers lengthwise into broad strips about 1¼ in/3 cm wide and then place in a colander, sprinkling each layer with a little salt. Leave to drain and release more liquid for at least 1 hour: this makes the peppers more digestible and gives them a deliciously mild flavor. ✌ Place the garlic in a small saucepan with the oil and cook gently over a very low heat for 3–5 minutes; do not let them color. ✌ Add the anchovies, crushing them with a wooden fork or spoon so that they dissolve in the oil. Leave over the heat for another 2 minutes. ✌ Transfer the bell peppers to a serving dish and sprinkle with the anchovy dressing. ✌ Serve at room temperature.

Insalata di Pollo
Chicken Salad

Serves 4
Preparation: 10 minutes
Recipe grading: easy

- 1 whole chicken breast, poached in chicken stock
- 2 anchovy fillets
- 4–5 tablespoons extra-virgin olive oil
- 1 tablespoon lemon juice
- salt to taste
- freshly ground white pepper
- 1 fresh white Alba truffle (optional)

Suggested wine: a dry, fruity white (Roero Arneis)

Cut the chicken breast into thin strips and place in a mixing bowl. ☙ Crumble the anchovy fillets with a fork and mix with the oil, lemon juice, salt, and white pepper in a small bowl until well blended. ☙ Pour over the chicken. ☙ Transfer to a serving dish and top with wafer-thin slices of fresh truffle, if liked.

When available, truffles add a touch of class to this simple but perfect salad.

Pomodori al Verde

Tomatoes with Green Sauce

Serves 4

Preparation: 20–25 minutes + at least 30 minutes' standing

Recipe grading: easy

Cut the tomatoes in half horizontally. Remove the seeds (but not the fleshy divisions between the seed chambers), then leave upside down to drain in a colander for 5–10 minutes. ❧ Fill each tomato half with Green Sauce. Arrange the tomatoes on a serving dish and serve. ❧ For a slightly richer dish, add mayonnaise to the green sauce. Allow about ¹/₂ tablespoon of mayonnaise for each half tomato.

- 4–8 medium ripe tomatoes
- 1 quantity Green Sauce (see recipe, page 15)

Suggested wine: a dry, lightly sparkling red (Freisa d'Asti)

This simple dish is best during the summer months when tomatoes are at their tastiest and best.

Tonno di Coniglio
Tunny Rabbit

Place the rabbit (in one piece) in a saucepan of boiling water without any salt. Add the cleaned and coarsely chopped carrot, onion, celery, and parsley. ❧ When the rabbit has boiled gently for 45 minutes, or when the flesh comes away from the bones easily, take it out of the cooking liquid. ❧ As soon as it is cool enough to handle, tear the flesh into pieces about 1¼ in/3 cm long (be sure to discard all the bones). ❧ Arrange the rabbit pieces in a bowl in two or three layers, alternating them with layers of whole garlic cloves and half the sage leaves. Sprinkle each layer with salt and white pepper to taste, then drizzle with the oil. ❧ Cover the bowl with a plate or with plastic wrap (cling film) and refrigerate for 24–36 hours. ❧ Two or three hours before serving, take the rabbit out of the refrigerator and let it come to room temperature. ❧ Arrange the rabbit mixture in a serving dish (including the garlic), but replace the sage leaves used to flavor the rabbit with 10 fresh ones.

Serves 4

Preparation: 15 minutes + 24–36 hours' chilling

Cooking: 45 minutes

Recipe grading: easy

- 1 rabbit, skinned, gutted and without head and feet, (weighing about 1¼ lb/ 625 g)
- 1 carrot
- 1 medium onion
- 1 stalk celery
- 3 sprigs parsley
- 10 cloves garlic, peeled and whole
- 20 fresh sage leaves
- salt to taste
- freshly ground white pepper
- ½ cup/4 fl oz/125 ml extra-virgin olive oil

Suggested wine: a young, dry red (Dolcetto d'Acqui)

This old-fashioned recipe from the limestone massif of Monferrato seems to have been forgotten by modern cooks, but it deserves to be revived. The name describes how the rabbit becomes as tender as tuna fish canned in oil. If you can't get rabbit, substitute the same quantity of chicken.

Primi piatti

Spaghetti and other types of dried, store-bought pasta are not typical of Piedmontese cuisine. The two traditional pasta dishes are *Agnolotti* (Stuffed pasta) served in boiling stock or with simple butter and herb sauces, and thinly sliced tagliatelle, known in the local dialect as *Tajarin*. Rice is the main ingredient in a wide variety of first courses; it is usually served with stock and vegetables in soups or made into delicious, subtly flavored risottos. As in many parts of northern Italy, where corn is widely grown, polenta is often served. *Gnocchi* (potato dumplings), common throughout Italy, are typically served with tasty fontina cheese or butter sauces in this region.

Minestra di Riso e Spinaci

Spinach and Rice Soup

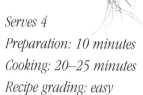

Wash the spinach leaves thoroughly. Drain briefly and place in a saucepan. Cover tightly and cook over a moderate heat for 2–3 minutes with just the water left clinging to the leaves. ❧ Remove from the heat and, when cool enough to handle, squeeze out as much moisture as possible. Chop coarsely. ❧ Melt the butter in the same saucepan, then add the spinach and a dash of salt. Cook over a moderate heat for 3 minutes while stirring and turning. Set aside. ❧ Bring the stock to a boil in a large saucepan. Add the rice and cook for 13–15 minutes. ❧ Add the prepared spinach. ❧ Beat the egg lightly in a bowl with salt and white pepper. Add the parmesan, then pour into the hot soup while beating with a balloon whisk. Turn off the heat. ❧ Leave to stand for 30 seconds before serving.

Serves 4
Preparation: 10 minutes
Cooking: 20–25 minutes
Recipe grading: easy

- 12 oz/350 g net weight, washed, trimmed fresh spinach leaves
- 2 tablespoons/1 oz/30 g butter
- salt to taste
- 4¼ cups/1¾ pints/1 liter meat stock (homemade or bouillon cube)
- 1 cup/7 oz/200 g Italian Arborio rice
- 1 egg
- freshly ground white pepper
- 3 tablespoons freshly grated parmesan cheese

Suggested wine: a fragrant, dry red (Grignolino del Monferrato Casalese)

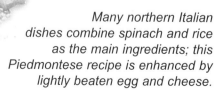

Many northern Italian dishes combine spinach and rice as the main ingredients; this Piedmontese recipe is enhanced by lightly beaten egg and cheese.

Zuppa alla Canavesana
Winter Cabbage Soup

Serves 4
Preparation: 15 minutes
Cooking: about an hour
Recipe grading: easy

Place the pork fat, butter, and garlic in a large heavy-bottomed saucepan and fry very gently over a low heat. ❧ Add the savoy cabbage and cook while stirring and turning for 7–8 minutes until it has wilted. ❧ Add the stock and simmer for 40 minutes. ❧ Season with salt and pepper. ❧ Place a layer of toasted bread slices in the bottom of a deep, earthenware pot or casserole. Sprinkle with some of the parmesan and pour about 1½ cups /12 fl oz /350 ml of the soup on top. Repeat this process until you have used all the ingredients. ❧ Bake in a preheated oven at 350°F/180°C/ gas 4 for 5–10 minutes before serving.

- 3 oz/90 g fresh or salted pork fat
- 2 tablespoons/1 oz/30 g butter
- 3 cloves garlic, finely chopped
- 1½ lb/750 g net weight, shredded savoy cabbage
- 4¼ cups/1¾ pints/1 liter boiling stock (homemade or bouillon cube)
- salt to taste
- freshly ground black pepper
- 4–8 slices of 2 or 3 day-old coarse white bread, toasted
- 8 tablespoons freshly grated parmesan cheese

Suggested wine: a dry white (Erbaluce)

For a heartier soup, fry the bread in butter instead of toasting it. For an equally delicious soup, substitute the savoy cabbage with the same quantity of thinly sliced young turnips. They will take about 30 minutes to cook.

Risotto alla Piemontese

Piedmontese Risotto

Serves 4
Preparation: 5 minutes
Cooking: 25 minutes
Recipe grading: fairly easy

Serves 4
Preparation: 5 minutes
Cooking: 25 minutes
Recipe grading: fairly easy

- 4 tablespoons/2 oz/60 g butter
- 2 tablespoons very finely chopped onion
- 1²/₃ cups/12 oz/350 g Italian Arborio rice
- ½ cup/4 fl oz/125 ml dry white wine
- 4¼ cups/1¾ pints/1 liter boiling stock (homemade or bouillon cube)
- ¾ cup/3 oz/90 g freshly grated parmesan cheese
- salt to taste
- freshly ground white pepper
- 3 tablespoons cooking juices from roast meat or poultry
- very thinly sliced fresh white truffles (optional)

Suggested wine: a dry, fruity white
(Langhe Riesling Renano)

Melt half the butter in a heavy-bottomed saucepan. Add the onion, then cover and cook over a gentle heat until it is soft and transparent. ❧ Add the rice and cook, stirring continuously, for 3–4 minutes. ❧ Sprinkle the wine over the rice and as soon as it has evaporated, add about ½ cup/4 fl oz/125 ml of the boiling stock. ❧ Continue cooking and stirring until it has been absorbed, then add more. Repeat this process until the rice has cooked for 15 minutes, adding smaller amounts of stock as the cooking progresses. ❧ Stir in half the parmesan and season with salt and pepper to taste. ❧ Continue cooking, but test a few grains of rice at frequent intervals to decide when it is ready. The rice should be just tender with a little "bite" left in it. ❧ Turn off the heat, then cover tightly and leave to stand for about 2 minutes to finish cooking. ❧ Dot the surface of the rice with the remaining butter, in thin slivers. Sprinkle with the remaining cheese and stir quickly but gently. ❧ Add the roast meat juices and stir once more. ❧ Serve at once on preheated plates, with shavings of truffle, if liked.

This risotto tastes wonderful when topped with Cheese Fondue (see recipe, page 24), with or without the final sprinkling of wafer-thin truffle slices.

Zuppa Mitunn
Bread and Cheese Soup

Place the slices of bread in a moderately hot oven to toast. They should be ³/₄ in/2 cm thick and about 3½ in/9 cm square. ❧ When the slices are crisp, rub them all over with the garlic. Arrange them in the bottom of a deep earthenware pot or casserole in layers, alternating with the Gruyère slices. Sprinkle with salt and pepper to taste. ❧ Slowly pour in sufficient stock to completely cover the topmost layer of toast. ❧ Place in a preheated oven at 400°F/200°C/gas 6 for 15 minutes. The toast should absorb all the stock during cooking. ❧ Serve at once.

Serves 4
Preparation: 15 minutes
Cooking: 15 minutes
Recipe grading: easy

- 8 slices of coarse-textured white bread
- 2 cloves garlic, peeled
- 7 oz/200 g thinly sliced Gruyère cheese
- salt to taste
- freshly ground black pepper
- about 5 cups/2 pints/generous 1 liter boiling stock (homemade or bouillon cube)

Suggested wine: a dry red (Dolcetto d'Asti)

The delicious stock leftover when making Mixed Boiled Meats (see recipe, page 64) is used as the basis for many first courses. Mixed with bread or rice it gives a superb flavor to many simple and satisfying soups and risottos.

Agnolotti
Stuffed Pasta with Sage and Butter Sauce

Serves 4

Preparation: 1¼ hours + 2–12 hours' resting for the pasta dough

Cooking: about 10 minutes

Recipe grading: complicated

FOR THE PASTA DOUGH:
- 1 quantity pasta dough (see recipe, page 51)

FOR THE FILLING:
- 2 tablespoons/1 oz/30 g butter
- 3 tablespoons cooking juices from roast meat (optional)
- ¾ cup/3 oz/90 g very finely chopped savoy cabbage leaves
- white part of a small leek, finely chopped
- 2 oz/60 g fresh Italian sausage meat (optional)
- 6 oz/180 g each, lean roast beef and pork
- 1 egg
- 2 tablespoons freshly grated parmesan cheese
- freshly grated nutmeg
- salt to taste
- freshly ground white pepper

FOR THE SAUCE:
- 4 tablespoons/2 oz/60 g butter
- 6 fresh sage leaves
- 4 tablespoons freshly grated parmesan cheese

Suggested wine: a light, dry red (Grignolino)

Prepare the pasta as explained on page 51. ❧ Melt the butter for the filling in a saucepan over a moderate heat. Add the meat juices, cabbage, leek, and the crumbled sausage meat (if using). Cook for 5–6 minutes, stirring frequently and moistening, if necessary, with a little stock or water. ❧ Leave to cool before grinding (mincing) twice, together with the roast meat. ❧ Place the finely ground mixture in a mixing bowl and add the egg, parmesan, a dash of nutmeg, salt, and white pepper. Mix very thoroughly, then set aside. ❧ Roll out the pasta dough until it is very thin. Use the reserved flour to sprinkle over the work surface and rolling pin to prevent the dough sticking. Cut the dough into 4 in/10 cm wide strips. ❧ Using a teaspoon or a pastry bag with a tip (nozzle), place small mounds of filling (about the size of a marble) lengthwise down the center of one half of each strip, spaced about 2 in/5 cm apart. ❧ Moisten the edges of the pasta strips and fold lengthwise in half to cover the filling, pinching the edges together and pressing down between the mounds to seal. ❧ Divide these long filled strips into separate agnolotti, cutting between the mounds with a fluted pastry wheel or cutter to make little stuffed pasta "pillows." ❧ Spread the agnolotti out in a single layer on a lightly floured clean cloth. Leave them to dry in a cool place for at least 2 hours, or overnight. ❧ Cook the agnolotti in plenty of boiling salted water for 3–5 minutes. ❧ Drain very thoroughly and transfer to a heated serving dish. ❧ Heat the butter and sage until golden brown and drizzle over the agnolotti. Sprinkle with the parmesan and serve hot.

The filling for the agnolotti varies greatly from place to place. One particularly prized filling uses chopped ham and truffle trimmings, while the sauce is a mixture of butter, wafer-thin slices of fresh white truffle, and parmesan. In some restaurants Agnolotti are now served with Cheese Fondue *(see recipe, page 20).*

Truffles: Piedmontese Gold

Truffles have been considered a delicacy in Italy since Roman times, although the truffles the ancients gorged on were not the same variety so treasured today. The Romans ate African truffles (which are nowhere near as good as those that grow on the Italian peninsula), and seemed to be unaware of the rich local stocks. Apicicus – a Roman cook, and author of the oldest surviving cook book – lists several recipes for truffles. In the Middle Ages they seemed to have been considered an evil food, or at best, a medicine, but had made a triumphant comeback by the early 13th century when they became very popular with the wealthy. Even Petrarch exalts their unique flavor in one of his poems. By Renaissance times truffles were *de rigueur* on all the best tables. Lucrezia Borgia loved truffles and Catherine de' Medici, the young Florentine woman who became queen of France, encouraged their use in French cuisine. During the 19th century truffles were the gastronomic symbol of refinement and wealth. Napoleon was crazy about them, as were his rivals, so much so that they were served at lunch during the Congress of Vienna in 1815 when Europe was reorganized after the Napoleonic Wars.

Because truffles grow underground, at depths of up to 12 in/30 cm, they are not easy to find. Only a few rare individuals are sufficently sensitive to the distinctive odor to locate them and truffle hunting is usually carried on with the aid of specially trained dogs or pigs. Being a truffle hunter, or trifolau, *as they are known in the local dialect, is an old and respected profession. The job calls for an exceptional knowledge of the local woods and conditions, plus a very well-trained dog or pig. The most common truffle dogs in Piedmont are setters crossbred with other hunting dogs. They are trained from six months onward.*

Truffles are a kind of subterranean fungus that grow mainly in temperate regions. They flourish in open woodlands and usually grow around the roots of certain trees, such as beech, willows, limes, and poplars. The white Piedmontese variety has a smooth surface while the black variety, more typical of central Italy, has a warty black surface.

The white truffles from Alba in Piedmont are considered among the best in the world. They mature between October and December and the highest quality specimens are sold for as much as $2000 each! In traditional circles, Alba truffles are served raw in very fine slices with only four local dishes – Eggs cooked in butter, Piedmontese Risotto (see recipe, page 44), Alba-style raw veal salad, and on Agnolotti (see recipe, page 46).

Truffles are the symbol of the city of Alba, one of the most important gastronomic towns in Italy. Every year a very important market is held and connoisseurs from far and wide flock to the town to see and buy the season's best. During the 60s and 70s the city sought world fame by sending the largest truffle found each year as a gift to well-known international personalities, from Sophia Loren to Harry Truman and Nikita Kruschev.

Tajarin

Tagliatelle in Rosemary and Butter Sauce

Serves 4

Preparation: 30 minutes + 1½ hours' resting time

Cooking: 2–3 minutes

Recipe grading: fairly easy

FOR THE PASTA:

- 3½ cups/14 oz/400 g unbleached, all-purpose/strong plain flour
- 2 eggs (at room temperature)
- 1 tablespoon extra-virgin olive oil
- ½ cup/3½ fl oz/100 ml cold water
- salt to taste

FOR THE ROSEMARY BUTTER:

- 2–3 tablespoons freshly grated parmesan cheese
- 4 tablespoons/2 oz/60 g butter
- 1 sprig fresh rosemary (or a sprig of fresh sage)
- wafer-thin slices of fresh white truffle

Suggested wine: a young, dry red (Roero)

To make the pasta dough: reserve about 2 tablespoons of the flour and heap up the rest in a mound on a pastry slab or work surface. Make a well in the center. ❧ Beat the eggs lightly with a fork in a bowl with the oil and water, then pour into the well. The amount of water needed will vary, depending on the absorbency of the flour. To be on the safe side, add only three-quarters of the amount given. After 2–3 minutes it will be obvious if you need to add the rest (you may even need more). ❧ Using a fork, gradually stir the egg mixture into the flour which will come away from the sides of the "well." ❧ When most of the flour has been absorbed, begin working the mixture by hand. Combine any remaining flour into the dough and knead thoroughly. Take time and energy over this stage. When well kneaded, the pasta dough will be smooth and elastic and will come cleanly away from the work surface. ❧ Form the dough into a ball and wrap in a clean cloth. Set aside to rest for 20–30 minutes at room temperature. ❧ Sprinkle a work surface with the reserved flour and roll the dough out into a very thin sheet. ❧ Roll the sheet of dough up loosely like a jelly roll (Swiss roll). Cut into slices about ¼ in/5 mm thick. (If using a pasta machine, set the cutters to this width.) ❧ Unravel the long, thin strips of pasta and spread them out on a cloth to dry for at least an hour. ❧ Cook the tagliatelle in a large pot of boiling salted water for 2–3 minutes. ❧ Drain well, then transfer to a heated serving dish. Sprinkle with the grated parmesan cheese. ❧ While the pasta is cooking, heat the butter and rosemary until the butter turns pale, golden brown. Drizzle the hot butter over the tagliatelle and toss gently. ❧ Top with slivers of fresh truffle and serve hot.

Cooking juices (left in the pan after roasting beef, pork, or poultry) sprinkled with a little freshly grated parmesan are another traditional sauce for the tagliatelle.

Cannelloni alla Barbaroux
Baked Stuffed Crêpes

Serves 4
Preparation: about 1 hour
Cooking: about 35 minutes
Recipe grading: complicated

FOR THE CRÊPES:
- 1 large egg
- ³/₄ cup/3 oz/90 g all-purpose/plain flour
- ²/₃ cup/5 fl oz/150 ml milk
- 3 tablespoons extra-virgin olive oil
- salt to taste

FOR THE FILLING:
- 8 oz/250 g lean roast veal
- 2¹/₂ oz/75 g Italian prosciutto
- 1 egg
- 1 tablespoon freshly grated parmesan cheese

FOR THE BÉCHAMEL SAUCE:
- 2 tablespoons/1 oz/30 g butter, plus a little extra for greasing
- ¹/₄ cup/1 oz/30 g all-purpose/plain flour
- 1 cup/8 fl oz/250 ml milk
- 1 tablespoon freshly grated parmesan cheese
- salt to taste
- freshly ground white pepper

Suggested wine: a dry, full-bodied red (Grignolino del Monferrato Casalese)

Prepare the crêpes. Break the egg into a mixing bowl and beat in the flour, milk, ¹/₂ tablespoon of the olive oil, and salt, using a balloon whisk or an electric beater. The batter should be smooth, with no lumps. ᕫ Heat 1 teaspoon of the oil in a nonstick skillet (frying pan) with a base diameter of 4 in/10 cm. Pour in 2 tablespoons of the batter and quickly tip the skillet this way and that to distribute the batter evenly over the bottom. The crêpe should be very thin; use a spatula to turn it after 40–50 seconds and cook for about 30 seconds or until the second side is golden brown. Slide the crêpe onto a plate. ᕫ Add another teaspoon of olive oil to the skillet and repeat the operation until all the batter has been used. The batter should yield 12 crêpes. ᕫ Prepare the filling. Grind (mince) the veal and prosciutto together finely and mix very thoroughly in a bowl with the egg and parmesan. ᕫ Spread some of this filling onto each crêpe and roll them up, not too tightly. ᕫ Place the filled crêpes in a fairly shallow ovenproof dish, greased with butter. ᕫ Prepare the béchamel sauce. Melt the butter in a small saucepan. Stir in the flour, and cook while stirring with a wooden spoon over a moderate heat for 2–3 minutes until pale golden brown. ᕫ Add the milk a little at a time, stirring continuously, and continue cooking while stirring for 5 minutes or a little longer, until the sauce has a very smooth pouring consistency. ᕫ Turn off the heat, then add the grated cheese and continue stirring for 1 minute. Season to taste with salt and white pepper. ᕫ Pour the béchamel over the stuffed crêpes. ᕫ Bake in a preheated oven at 400°F/200°C/gas 6 until the the surface is light, golden brown. ᕫ Serve piping hot.

The Cheeses of Piedmont and Aosta

The alpine valleys of Piedmont and Val d'Aosta are ideal for milk production. Traditional cooking in these regions is based in large part on milk and milk products, such as butter and cheese. Fontina is probably the most well-known cheese. It takes its name from the alpine area called Font, where the highest quality milk is said to be

produced. The earliest records of fontina cheese date back to the 13th century. Genuine fontina is DOC (*denominazione di origine controllata*, an Italian warrant of quality for agricultural products) and, since 1996, is also DOP (*denominazione di origine protetta*, which is a European warrant of quality and production standards).

Gorgonzola is a very ancient cheese. It was first made in Lombardy, in the little town of Gorgonzola, just a few miles from Milan, but passed to Piedmont early in the 20th century. It is made in the Novara province from cow's milk. During aging holes are made in the forms of cheese to encourage the growth of the characteristic blue-green mold. It has a pungent foretaste with a creamy, sweet background aroma.

Robiola is a fresh cheese traditionally made of goat's milk only. It is a soft spreadable cheese, with a delicate perfume and a slightly sharp taste.

Toma is an ancient word for cheese made with whole (full cream) milk. It is made high in the mountains with cow's milk and a very small quantity of sheep's and goat's milk. Tomini are small, fresh cheeses made with cow's milk or a mixture of cow's and goat's or sheep's milk.

Sheep, goats, and cows have been kept in Piedmont and the Val d'Aosta for hundreds of years. Many of the cheese-making processes have remained unchanged through the centuries.

Fontina cheese is made in the Val d'Aosta using cow's milk; 10 quarts (10 liters) of milk are required to obtain two pounds (one kilo) of cheese. Fontina is aged in underground caves at a constant temperature of 25°F (10°C) and with high humidity (about 90 percent). The rind is salted every second day for at least three months. When mature, the amber-colored rind is thin and the cheese itself melts in the mouth. Fontina is mainly used for cooking, and is served as fondue, with gnocchi or polenta, and with bread and rice soups.

Gnocchi di Cuneo

Cuneo Potato Dumplings

Serves 4
Preparation: 25 minutes
Cooking: 2 minutes
Recipe grading: fairly easy

- 1½ lb/750 g white, floury potatoes
- 3 eggs, separated
- 1¼ cups/5 oz/150 g all-purpose/plain flour
- salt to taste
- freshly ground white pepper
- freshly grated nutmeg
- 4 tablespoons freshly grated parmesan cheese
- 4 tablespoons/2 oz/60 g butter
- 5–6 fresh sage leaves

Suggested wine: a dry white (Roero Arneis)

Scrub the potatoes with a vegetable brush under cold running water. Boil until tender, then peel them. Put them through a potato ricer into a mixing bowl while they are still hot. ❧ Beat the egg whites in a large mixing bowl until stiff. Then gently fold in the yolks, flour, salt and pepper to taste, a dash of nutmeg, and, finally, the potatoes. Mix gently but thoroughly. ❧ Bring a large saucepan of salted water to the boil and drop small rounded tablespoonfuls of the potato mixture into the boiling water. When the dumplings bob up to the surface, they are done. Use a slotted ladle or spoon to take them out as soon as they are ready. ❧ Transfer to a heated serving dish and sprinkle with the parmesan. Melt the butter and sage together in a small saucepan until the butter is pale golden brown. ❧ Drizzle the flavored butter all over the dumplings and serve immediately.

These potato dumplings are called "dunderet" in the local dialect. They differ slightly from classic gnocchi for their shape. They are a classic dish for feast days in Cuneo.

Riso ai Formaggi

Rice with Four Cheeses

Cook the rice in plenty of boiling salted water for 10–12 minutes or until only just tender. Drain briefly (it should still be moist) and place in a bowl. ❧ Mix the rice with half the butter, three-quarters of the parmesan, a dash of nutmeg (if liked), salt, and white pepper. ❧ Melt 1 tablespoon/½ oz /15 g of the butter in a large, nonstick skillet (frying pan). Add the rice and cook, stirring continuously, for 3–4 minutes over a moderate heat; this will bring out the flavors and finish cooking the rice. ❧ Transfer one-third of the rice to a greased, deep ovenproof dish. Sprinkle this first rice layer with half each of the fontina, gruyère, and provolone cheeses. Cover with half the remaining rice and sprinkle with the remaining cheeses. ❧ Top with a final layer of rice and sprinkle with the remaining parmesan. Melt the remaining butter and drizzle over the rice. ❧ Bake in a preheated oven at 375°F/190°C/gas 5 for 15–20 minutes.

Serves 4
Preparation: 15 minutes
Cooking: 30–35 minutes
Recipe grading: easy

- 1⅔ cups/12 oz/350 g Italian Arborio rice
- 6 tablespoons 3 oz/90 g butter, chopped
- ½ cup/2 oz/60 g freshly grated parmesan cheese
- freshly grated nutmeg (optional)
- salt to taste
- freshly grated white pepper
- a little extra butter for greasing the ovenproof dish
- ½ cup/2½ oz/75 g coarsely grated fontina cheese
- ½ cup/2½ oz/75 g coarsely grated gruyère cheese
- ½ cup/2½ oz/75 g coarsely grated provolone cheese

Suggested wine: a dry, almondy red (Val d'Aosta Donnas)

In the Cuneo district tagliatelle ("tajarin" in the local dialect) are prepared in the same way: cooked in boiling salted water until barely tender, they are then baked in the oven for about 5–7 minutes.

Polenta con Salsa di Porri
Polenta with Leek Sauce

Serves 4
Preparation: 15 minutes
Cooking: about 1 hour
Recipe grading: easy

FOR THE POLENTA:

- 6½ cups/2½ pints/1.5 liters cold water
- scant tablespoon coarse salt
- 2¼ cups/12 oz/350 g coarse-grain yellow cornmeal

FOR THE SAUCE:

- 12 oz/350 g leeks, prepared net weight, white part only
- 3 tablespoons/1½ oz/45 g butter
- salt to taste
- freshly ground white pepper
- 1½ cups/10 fl oz/300 ml light/single cream
- 4–5 tablespoons whole/full cream milk

Suggested wine: a dry, lightly sparkling red (Barbera del Monferrato Vivace)

Polenta used to be cooked in a traditional copper kettle suspended over a wood fire. Making polenta is hard work and nowadays many Italians use electric polenta cookers. Another alternative is to buy the new quick-cook cornmeals which only require 8–10 minutes cooking (and stirring!).

Bring the water to a boil with the salt. Gradually sprinkle in the cornmeal while stirring continuously with a large balloon whisk to stop lumps from forming. ❧ Cook over a low heat, stirring continuously for about 45 minutes. ❧ Cut the prepared leeks into ⅛ in/2–3 mm thick slices. ❧ Melt the butter in a saucepan over a moderate heat, then add the leeks. Cover and cook gently for 5 minutes, or until they have wilted. ❧ Season to taste with salt and white pepper. Add the cream and milk and cook for 20–25 minutes. ❧ When the polenta is done (it should be very thick, almost stiff), turn it out onto a heated serving platter. ❧ Serve hot with the leek sauce handed round separately in another heated serving dish.

Gnocchi alla Fontina

Potato Dumplings with Melted Fontina Cheese

Serves 4–6

Preparation: 35 minutes + 1–2 hours' resting

Cooking: 25 minutes

Recipe grading: fairly easy

- 2 lb/1 kg white, floury potatoes
- 2 cups/8 oz/250 g all-purpose/plain flour + 3–4 tablespoons extra
- 1 teaspoon salt
- scant 2 cups/7 oz/200 g coarsely grated fontina cheese
- 4 tablespoons/2 oz/60 g butter, melted and golden brown

Suggested wine: a dry almondy red (Barmet)

Scrub the potatoes with a vegetable brush under cold running water. Boil until tender, then peel them. Put them through a potato ricer into a mixing bowl while they are still hot. ❧ Stir in the flour and salt to make a soft, homogenous mixture that holds its shape. ❧ Sprinkle the work surface lightly with some of the extra flour. Using a quarter of the dough, shape it into long rolls about as thick as your thumb. Cut these into segments just under ³/₄ in/2 cm long. ❧ Press each dumpling one by one against the prongs of a fork (concave side) with your thumb, so that they are slightly hollowed out on one side and ribbed on the other. ❧ Repeat with the remaining dough, spreading the gnocchi out on a lightly floured cloth as you shape them. ❧ Leave the gnocchi to rest for at least 1–2 hours. ❧ Bring a large saucepan of salted water to a boil and add all the gnocchi at once. Use a slotted spoon to remove them in batches as they bob up to the surface. This will take about 2–4 minutes. ❧ Drain well and transfer to a heated serving dish. Sprinkle with the cheese, drizzle with the butter, and serve at once.

Polenta di Frumentino

Polenta with Buckwheat Flour, Anchovies, and Cheese

Bring the water to a boil with the coarse salt. Sprinkle in the cornmeal and the buckwheat flour, stirring continuously with a balloon whisk to prevent any lumps forming. ❧ Cook over a moderate heat, stirring almost continuously for 45 minutes or, better still, 1 hour. ❧ When the polenta is ready (it should be stiff), turn it out onto a platter or cutting board and let it cool for 30 minutes or longer. ❧ Melt three-quarters of the butter in a small saucepan. ❧ Use the remaining butter to grease a fairly deep ovenproof dish. ❧ Cut the polenta into pieces about ³/₄ in/2 cm thick. Place a layer of polenta pieces (use about one-third) in the greased dish and sprinkle with about one-third of the anchovies, cheese slices, and melted butter. Repeat the operation, using half the remaining polenta, all the remaining anchovies and cheese slices, and about half the remaining melted butter. ❧ Cover with a final layer of polenta and drizzle the remaining butter all over it. ❧ Bake in a preheated oven at 400°F/200°C/gas 6 for about 20–25 minutes, until golden brown on top.

Serves 4

Preparation: 25 minutes + 30 minutes resting

Cooking: 80 minutes

Recipe grading: easy

- 6¹/₂ cups/2¹/₂ pints/1.5 liters water
- 1 tablespoon coarse sea salt
- 1¹/₄ cups/7 oz/200 g coarse-grain yellow cornmeal/polenta
- 1¹/₄ cups/5 oz/150 g buckwheat flour
- ¹/₂ cup/4 oz/125 g butter
- 3¹/₂ oz/100 g salted anchovies, rinsed and boned
- generous 8 oz/250 g fresh toma (or fontina) cheese

Suggested wine: a dry, full-bodied red (Gattinara)

Buckwheat flour is never used on its own in Piedmontese cooking, but is mixed with cornmeal (polenta) or, sometimes, with cooked, sieved potatoes.

Secondi piatti

Meat is still the chief component of the main course and the central dish of any important meal. The range of meat available is wide, from the game hunted in the upland valleys and rolling woodlands, to the beef, chicken, and rabbits commonly kept by farmers. Salami and other cured meats and sausages are also widely made. Meat is often cooked in butter, cream, or cheese, or is slowly braised in the region's full-bodied, dry red wines. But the pride of Piedmont's restaurants even today is still the array of boiled or roast meats wheeled out on a trolley so that diners can choose their favorite pieces which are then carved off before their eyes.

Spezzatino alla Panna
Veal and Cream Casserole

Season the meat lightly with a little salt and pepper. ❧ Heat a quarter of the butter in a fireproof casserole until it stops foaming. Add the veal and brown, stirring frequently for 10–15 minutes over a moderate heat. ❧ While the meat is browning, melt the remaining butter in a small saucepan. Add the flour and stir with a wooden spoon while cooking over a moderate heat for 2 minutes or until it starts to color. Add the flour mixture to the meat and cook for a few minutes, stirring continuously. ❧ Pour in the cream, then cover. Simmer over a low heat for at least 1 hour, stirring now and then. ❧ If the liquid reduces too much, add 2 tablespoons of milk or water. There should be plenty of sauce. ❧ Taste and add more salt if necessary. Serve hot.

Serves 4
Preparation: 5 minutes
Cooking: about 1½ hours
Recipe grading: easy

- 1¼ lb/625 g veal, shank or shoulder, cut into 1¼ in/3 cm cubes
- salt to taste
- freshly ground white pepper
- 4 tablespoons/2 oz/60 g butter
- 1–2 tablespoons all-purpose/plain flour
- 1½ cups/12 fl oz/375 ml light/single cream

Suggested wine: a dry rosé
(Rosé di Fontanarossa)

This classic dish is particularly good when served with boiled new potatoes.

Baié
Mixed Boiled Meats

Serves 10

Preparation: 10 minutes

Cooking: 4 hours or longer

Recipe grading: easy

- about 6 quarts/10 pints/6 liters cold water
- 4–6 cloves (optional)
- 1½ large onions, peeled and trimmed
- 3 stalks celery, trimmed and washed
- 3 medium carrots, peeled
- about 20 black peppercorns
- 3 tablespoons coarse salt
- boneless beef cuts from brisket, bottom round/topside or rump roast/silverside, weighing 3½ lb/1.5 kg
- boneless veal cuts from breast or shoulder, weighing 2 lb/1 kg
- ½ oven-ready chicken (or ½ capon)
- 1¼ lb/625 g calf's tongue
- 1 cotechino sausage, weighing 1½ lb/ 750 g

Suggested wine: a dry red (Corvo rosso)

Mixed Boiled Meats *are served all over Italy, but the Piedmontese version is unrivalled in its abundance and variety, reflecting the excellent quality of locally produced meat. The cooking liquid from the veal and beef pot is an excellent stock which can be used to make soups, risottos, and many pasta dishes. It freezes well and can be used as required.*

Bring the water to a boil in a very large, deep saucepan. ❧ If using cloves, stick them into the onions. Add 1 onion, 2 stalks celery, 2 carrots, two-thirds of the peppercorns, and 2 tablespoons of the salt to the boiling water. ❧ Add the beef and when the water has returned to a boil, reduce the heat a little and cover. ❧ Simmer for 1 hour, then add the veal and the chicken (or capon). ❧ Cook for 2 more hours, topping up with boiling water if necessary. ❧ Test the meats after this time with a thin skewer: if they are not tender, continue simmering for another 30 minutes or longer. ❧ Meanwhile, in a separate pot, cook the calf's tongue with the remaining onion, celery, carrot, peppercorns, and salt. This will take about 2 hours to cook, so time it so that it is ready when the other meats are. Discard the stock from the tongue when done. ❧ Soak the cotechino sausage in plenty of cold water for 1 hour. Prick the skin with the tip of a wooden pick and place in a saucepan with enough fresh cold water to cover. Bring the water very slowly to a boil over a very low heat and simmer gently (the water should barely move). If allowed to boil, the sausage may burst. The sausage will take about 3 hours to cook. Discard the cooking liquid. ❧ Although all the meats should, ideally, be ready at the same time, they will not spoil if kept waiting in their cooking liquid for a little while until everything is done. ❧ Slice the cotechino sausage, but leave the other meats whole. Arrange on one or more preheated serving platters. Serve with a selection of sauces, including Green Sauce (see recipe, page 15), Warm Red Sauce (see recipe, page 16), Dijon-style mustard, or, more simply, a generous drizzling of the finest quality extra-virgin olive oil.

Costolette alla Valdostana
Veal Cutlets with Melted Cheese Filling

Serves 4
Preparation: 10 minutes
Cooking: 15–18 minutes
Recipe grading: easy

- 4 veal cutlets, each weighing about 6–7 oz/180–200 g
- 4 oz/125 g fontina cheese, thinly sliced
- wafer-thin slices of fresh truffle (optional)
- salt to taste
- freshly ground black pepper
- 1 tablespoon all-purpose/plain flour
- 1 egg, lightly beaten
- 5–6 tablespoons fine, dry breadcrumbs
- 7 tablespoons/3½ oz/100 g butter

Use a very sharp, pointed knife to cut horizontally into the meat of the cutlets toward the bone to form a pocket. ❧ Place a quarter of the fontina slices inside each pocket, together with a few slivers of truffle, if using. ❧ Beat the edges of the pockets lightly to make the cut edges stick together, enclosing the contents. ❧ Sprinkle the cutlets with a little salt and pepper and coat with flour. Dip them into the egg and then coat with breadcrumbs. ❧ Heat about two-thirds of the butter over a fairly high heat in a large, nonstick skillet (frying pan) until it stops foaming. Add the cutlets and fry until they are golden brown on both sides. Add the remaining butter (cut into small pieces) when you turn them. ❧ Serve very hot.

Suggested wine: a dry, full-bodied red (Barbaresco)

Tapilon
Braised Beef

Cook the garlic and rosemary in the oil and butter in a fireproof casserole over a moderate heat for 2 minutes. ❧ Add the beef, breaking it up with a fork. Cook for 5–7 minutes, stirring frequently, until all the meat changes color and the liquid it produces has evaporated. Season with salt and pepper. ❧ Add the bay leaf and half the wine and simmer gently over a low heat for 40 minutes. Stir now and then during cooking and gradually add the remaining wine. ❧ Serve hot with boiled rice or polenta (see recipe for polenta, page 58).

Serves 4
Preparation: 5 minutes
Cooking: about 1 hour
Recipe grading: easy

- 2 large cloves garlic, finely chopped
- 1 tablespoon freshly chopped rosemary leaves
- 4 tablespoons extra-virgin olive oil
- 3 tablespoons/1½ oz/45 g butter
- 5 cups/1¼ lb/625 g lean ground beef
- salt to taste
- freshly ground black pepper
- 1 bay leaf
- 1¼ cups/10 fl oz/300 ml full-bodied dry red wine

Suggested wine: a dry, full-bodied red (Gattinara)

This dish used to be made with donkey meat, cut into tiny pieces. Nowadays ground beef is used in its place.

Brasato al Barolo

Beef Braised in Red Wine

Serves 5–6
Preparation: 20 minutes
Cooking: 4 hours
Recipe grading: easy

Wrap the pork fat around the beef and tie with kitchen string. ❧ Sprinkle with salt and pepper, then coat lightly with flour. ❧ Heat the oil and butter in a fireproof casserole large enough to accommodate the meat snugly. When the oil and butter are sizzling, add the beef and brown all over. This will take about 10 minutes. ❧ Remove the meat from the casserole and set aside. ❧ Add the rosemary, sage, garlic, parsley, onion, carrot, and celery to the butter, oil, and juices left in the casserole. Sauté gently over a moderate heat for 5 minutes. ❧ Add the meat, bay leaves, cloves, and a dash of nutmeg, then moisten with 2–3 tablespoons of boiling water. Cook for 1 minute. ❧ Add 1 cup/8 fl oz/250 ml of the Barolo wine. Reduce the heat to low and cover the casserole tightly. When the liquid has reduced considerably (after about 40 minutes), add the remaining wine and continue cooking, covered, for 3 hours, turning the piece of beef at intervals. ❧ Test the meat with a thin metal skewer. When cooked, it should be very tender. ❧ Discard the bay leaves and cloves just before serving. Remove the beef and keep hot. ❧ Taste the cooking liquid, and add a little salt if necessary then strain through a fine sieve, pushing the vegetables through (or process in the blender until very smooth). ❧ Slice the beef about ¹/₂ in/1 cm thick. Transfer to a heated serving platter and cover with the sauce. ❧ Serve hot with polenta (see recipe, page 58) or potato purée.

- 2 slices pork fat, ¹/₂ in/1 cm thick
- 2 lb/1 kg beef, chuck or boneless rump roast/silverside
- salt to taste
- freshly ground black pepper
- 1–2 tablespoons all-purpose/plain flour
- 3 tablespoons extra-virgin olive oil
- 3 tablespoons/1¹/₂ oz/45 g butter
- ¹/₂ tablespoon finely chopped fresh rosemary leaves
- 4 sage leaves, finely chopped
- 1 clove garlic, finely chopped
- 1 teaspoon finely chopped parsley
- 1 medium onion, peeled and coarsely chopped
- 1 medium carrot, peeled and coarsely chopped
- 1 stalk celery, trimmed and sliced
- 2 bay leaves
- 1–2 cloves
- freshly ground nutmeg
- 1 bottle of Barolo wine

Suggested wine: a dry, full-bodied red (Barolo)

Superb Piedmontese beef and the best Barolo wine make this an exceptional dish. In days of old, the beef was marinated in Barolo wine with mixed herbs and spices for anything from 12 hours to 6–7 days. Next it was browned in butter and oil, then cooked in the marinade.

Rolata di Vitello

Veal Roll

Serves 4

Preparation: 15 minutes

Cooking: about 1 hour

Recipe grading: easy

- 1 piece of boned breast of veal, weighing about 1 lb/500 g
- 3½ oz/100 g fatty Italian prosciutto, sliced
- 1 tablespoon finely chopped fresh rosemary leaves
- 3 fresh sage leaves, finely chopped
- 2 cloves garlic, finely chopped
- salt to taste
- freshly ground white pepper
- 4 tablespoons/2 oz/60 g butter
- scant 1 cup/7 fl oz/200 ml dry white wine
- a little hot stock (homemade or bouillon cube), as required

Suggested wine: a dry red
(Grignolino d'Asti)

Use a meat bat (pounder) to flatten the breast of veal until it is just under ½ in/1 cm thick. Beat carefully to avoid tearing holes in the veal. ✍ Spread the slices of prosciutto over the veal and sprinkle with the rosemary, sage, garlic, salt, and pepper. ✍ Roll up the veal carefully and tie with kitchen string. Do not salt the outside. ✍ Heat the butter in a large fireproof casserole. When it has stopped foaming, add the meat and brown over a fairly high heat for 6–7 minutes. ✍ Add one-third of the wine, then reduce the heat a little and cover. ✍ Turn the meat at frequent intervals and add more wine as the liquid evaporates. Add a little stock, if necessary, when you have used up all the wine. ✍ After 45 minutes, the veal roll will be cooked. Turn off the heat and leave to rest in the casserole for 6–8 minutes. ✍ Remove the string and carve the roll into slices about ½ in/1 cm thick. ✍ Serve hot or at room temperature.

This classic braised dish is traditionally served with boiled spinach tossed in a little butter, and potato purée.

Vitello Tonnato

Veal with Tuna Sauce

Heat the oil in a fireproof casserole. When it is very hot, add the meat and brown over a high heat, turning frequently. ❧ Season with salt and pepper and pour in the wine. ❧ Cover the casserole and place in a preheated oven at 350°F/180°C/gas 4 for about 50 minutes. Turn the meat 2 or 3 times during cooking. ❧ When the veal is done, transfer to a large plate and leave to cool. ❧ Make the mayonnaise using the egg yolks, lemon juice to taste, and the olive oil. ❧ Finely chop the tuna, anchovy fillets, and half the capers. Stir this mixture into the mayonnaise. ❧ Taste and season with salt and pepper, if required. ❧ Cut the cold veal into thin slices and arrange these in a large, shallow serving dish. Spread the tuna mayonnaise over the top. ❧ Garnish with the remaining capers and chill in the refrigerator for an hour or so before serving.

Serves 4

Preparation: 20 minutes + 1 hour's chilling

Cooking: about 50 minutes

Recipe grading: fairly easy

- 3 tablespoons extra-virgin olive oil
- 1¼ lb/625 g top round of veal/boned leg of veal, firmly tied
- salt to taste
- freshly ground white pepper
- scant 1 cup/7 fl oz/200 ml dry white wine
- 1 bay leaf
- 1 clove garlic
- ½ stalk green celery

FOR THE SAUCE:

- 2 egg yolks (at room temperature)
- 2 tablespoons lemon juice
- scant 1 cup/7 fl oz/200 ml extra-virgin olive oil
- a 7 oz/200 g can of tuna in olive oil
- 4–6 anchovy fillets
- 2 tablespoons capers
- salt to taste
- freshly ground white pepper

This dish also makes an excellent appetizer (for 8 people). It can be made in advance and kept in the refrigerator. Take out of the refrigerator 1 hour before serving.

Suggested wine: a dry white (Gavi)

The Red Wines of Piedmont

The red wines of Piedmont have long been considered the best of their kind in Italy, and among the best in the world. Barolo, Barbaresco, Gattinara, Barbera, Freisa, Dolcetto, Grignolino, and Nebbiolo are among the best names. There is a tradition in Piedmont of making classic wines for important dishes and special occasions that will also age well. The most well-known is Barolo (once considered the

best red wine in Italy, an honor it now shares with the Tuscan Brunello di Montalcino), which has been described as "the king of wines, and a wine for kings." But many other Piedmont reds come close to Barolo in quality; Barbaresco (made from the same grape) is usually given as Barolo's strongest challenger. Barolo and Barbaresco are best served with roasted red meats and with mature cheeses.

Only slightly less great than Barolo and Barbaresco are Barbera, Carema, and Ghemme — also made from the Nebbiolo grape — along with Dolcetto, Freisa, Grignolino, and others. These are all potentially great wines, and their quality depends on the region they were produced in and who made them. In any case, they are almost always a good buy. Dolcetto is deep ruby in color with flashes of purple, its fragrance is slightly fruity. It does not age well and should be drunk young at room temperature. Grignolino is another wine that should be drunk while young. Gattinara merits special mention, since it is such a special wine, particularly if aged for four or more years. Like all the great Piedmontese reds, it is made from the nebbiolo grape. It has vastly improved over the last few years and may even come close in the near future to challenging Barolo and Barbaresco. Barbera d'Alba is a highly refined wine, with a delicate and fragrant perfume. It is best served with cured and roast meats and with mature cheeses.

While Piedmont is definitely not a paradise for lovers of dry white wine, one or two very drinkable whites can be found. Roero Arneis, made in the area around Asti, and Gavi or Cortese di Gavi, made in the western Monferrato hills, are both fine wines.

Barolo is aged for not less than three years, two of which must be in wood. A Barolo that has been aged for five years will have Riserva (reserve) on the label. A good Barolo should be opened at least ten hours before serving, while two hours will be sufficient for Barbaresco. Unlike most reds, a half bottle of Barolo opened two or three days earlier will often acquire extra fragrance and taste. Both wines have a fine, full fragrance, with a hint of violet. Tastewise, they are smooth, velvety and fairly austere, Barbaresco is slightly lighter, Barolo slightly fuller. Barolo and Barbaresco are both good "meditative" wines and should be served at a warmish room temperature.

Carbonade della Val d'Aosta

Beef Casserole from the Val d'Aosta

Serves 4
Preparation: 15 minutes
Cooking: about 1 hour
Recipe grading: easy

- 1¼ lb/625 g lean braising beef
- 2 tablespoons all-purpose/plain flour
- 4 tablespoons/2 oz/60 g butter
- 2 large onions, peeled and sliced
- salt to taste
- freshly ground black pepper
- 1¾ cups/14 fl oz/400 ml full-bodied, dry red wine

Suggested wine: a dry, full-bodied red
(Valle d'Aosta Chambave Rosso)

Cut the meat into very thin slices (it does not matter if their shapes vary). Coat lightly with flour. The easiest way to do this is to put the flour into a strong paper or plastic bag, then add the meat and hold the bag tightly closed as you shake it. ❧ Melt the butter in a fireproof casserole. Add the beef slices and brown all over, turning them frequently for 2 minutes over a fairly high heat. ❧ Remove the meat from the casserole with a slotted spoon and set aside. ❧ Add the onion to the butter and juices left in the casserole then sauté over a moderate heat until it is soft and lightly browned. ❧ Add the meat and stir. Season with salt and pepper and moisten with about a quarter of the wine. Simmer gently over a very low heat, uncovered, for 45–50 minutes, adding more wine at intervals. ❧ When cooked, there should be plenty of rich, dark liquid and the onion should have almost completely dissolved. ❧ Serve hot.

This dish used to be made with salted beef. Nowadays fresh beef is always used. It is traditionally served with freshly made polenta (see recipe, page 58), but is equally good with potato purée (mashed potatoes) or rice.

Puccia

Pork, Vegetable, and Polenta Casserole

Place the pork in a fireproof casserole with the savoy cabbage, onion, carrot, and celery. Add a dash of salt and the water. Cover tightly and bring quickly to a boil. ❧ Reduce the heat to moderate and simmer for 30 minutes. ❧ While the pork and vegetables are cooking, bring 5¼ cups/ generous 2 pints/1.25 liters of salted water to a boil in a large, heavy bottomed saucepan. Sprinkle in the cornmeal while stirring continuously with a large balloon whisk to prevent lumps forming. Continue cooking over a moderate heat, stirring almost continuously for 20–25 minutes. ❧ Add the meat, vegetables, and their cooking liquid to this very soft polenta and stir well. ❧ Simmer for 20–25 more minutes, stirring very frequently and adding a little boiling water when necessary to keep the polenta very moist and soft. ❧ Finally, stir in the butter and the parmesan. Serve immediately.

Serves 4
Preparation: 10 minutes
Cooking: about 1 hour
Recipe grading: easy

- 1 lb/500 g loin of pork, cut in 1¼-1½ in/3–4 cm cubes
- 1¼ lb/625 g savoy cabbage, cut into thin strips
- 1 small onion, thickly sliced
- 1 small carrot, sliced
- 1 stalk celery, sliced
- salt to taste
- ½ cup/4 fl oz/125 ml hot water
- 1½ cups/7 oz/200 g coarse-grain yellow cornmeal
- 5 tablespoons/2½ oz/75 g butter, cut into small pieces
- 4 tablespoons freshly grated parmesan cheese

Suggested wine: a dry, full-bodied red (Dolcetto d'Alba Superiore)

This hearty winter dish is typical of traditional peasant cooking in the Alba region. If any of this delicious casserole is leftover, slice when cold and firm. Then fry in plenty of very hot olive oil in a skillet (frying pan) over a high heat until crisp and golden brown. Drain briefly and serve immediately.

Giovanni Vialardi: Royal Chef at the Court of Savoy

Giovanni Vialardi was chef for the royal House of Savoy under kings Charles Albert and Victor Emmanuel II during the 19th century. Giovanni, who had received extensive training under both Italian and foreign chefs, was a talented and expert cook. Both Charles Albert and Victor Emmanuel had Austrian wives – Maria Teresa of Lorraine and Maria Adelaide of Austria – and for obvious reasons Giovanni's cooking had strong Austrian undertones. He was also heavily influenced by the French, whose growing middle classes were creating a new and more practical approach to a previously sumptuous and refined cuisine.

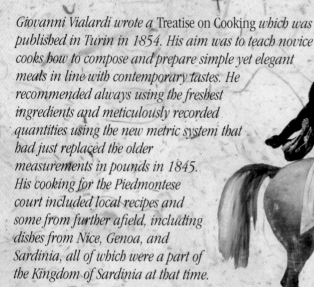

Giovanni Vialardi wrote a Treatise on Cooking which was published in Turin in 1854. His aim was to teach novice cooks how to compose and prepare simple yet elegant meals in line with contemporary tastes. He recommended always using the freshest ingredients and meticulously recorded quantities using the new metric system that had just replaced the older measurements in pounds in 1845. His cooking for the Piedmontese court included local recipes and some from further afield, including dishes from Nice, Genoa, and Sardinia, all of which were a part of the Kingdom of Sardinia at that time.

Left: an elaborately decorated room in the Palazzo Stupinigi, the royal villa of the Savoys.

Below: an eighteenth century diagram showing how to lay the table for an elegant dinner party.

The Treatise is composed of nineteen chapters with recipes for food and drinks, as well as tips on how to serve elaborate meals and banquets. The chapters are organized according to the types of food and the way they are served. Beginning with a series of recipes for babies and children, the Treatise goes on to list dishes for first courses, second courses, fish, and then a mixed meat chapter. Vialardi dedicated plenty of space to the latter, which was very fashionable at the time. They consisted of spectacular dishes made with cold meats, gelatin, butter, and vegetables and were designed to astonish and delight the royal banqueters.

Giovanni did not have an easy life under Victor Emmanuel II (above), who was reputedly both abrupt and awkward. He detested court banquets and refined food and preferred simple, even frugal meals.

The last three chapters of Vialardi's Treatise are dedicated to desserts and confectionery of all types, arts which the author particularly enjoyed. Here too, and according to the French fashions of the time, there are instructions on how to prepare astonishing compositions of multicolored foods; these dishes reflect the contemporary Romantic fashion for Renaissance times when very elaborate food was a symbol of the wealth and power of the Lord who could afford to serve it. The Treatise finishes with a brief encyclopedia on household management with tips for the modern housewife on a broad range of subjects, such as how to preserve food in the heat before the invention of refrigerators. The Treatise is written in an elegant French style. The precision and clarity of the instructions and the delightful drawings and illustrations which enliven its pages make it rather exceptional for its time.

Fagiano al Tartufo

Truffled Pheasant

Season the cavity of the pheasant with salt and pepper and place the juniper berries inside it. ❧ Wrap the slices of pancetta around the breast of the bird and secure these with kitchen string. Tie the legs and wings snugly against the bird's body so that it keeps its shape as it cooks. ❧ Heat the butter in a saucepan just large enough to contain the pheasant and brown the bird all over for 5 minutes, turning frequently. ❧ Add the onion, celery, sage, and rosemary. Pour the wine over the pheasant. Then cover and reduce the heat to fairly low. Cook for 40–45 minutes. ❧ Remove the pheasant when it is done and keep hot. ❧ Strain the cooking liquid and return it to the saucepan. Pour in the cream and simmer for 2–3 minutes, adding salt to taste. ❧ Remove the trussing string, pancetta, and juniper berries from the pheasant and carve it into 4 or more pieces. ❧ Add the pieces of pheasant to the sauce, turning once or twice to moisten and reheat. ❧ After a few minutes, transfer to a preheated serving dish. Spoon the sauce over the pheasant and garnish with the shavings of truffles, if using. ❧ Serve hot.

Serves 4
Preparation: 15 minutes
Cooking: about 1 hour
Recipe grading: easy

- 1 roasting pheasant
- salt to taste
- freshly ground white pepper
- 4 juniper berries, slightly crushed
- 4 slices unrolled Italian pancetta
- 2 tablespoons/1 oz/30 g butter
- 2 tablespoons coarsely chopped onion
- 1 stalk celery, coarsely chopped
- 3 fresh sage leaves
- 1 small sprig fresh rosemary
- generous ⅔ cup/5 fl oz/150 ml dry white wine
- scant ¼ cup/3½ fl oz/100 ml light/single cream
- 1 fresh truffle (optional), in wafer-thin slices

Suggested wine: a dry, full-bodied red (Barbera d'Alba)

Piedmontese Risotto *(see recipe, page 44) goes very well with the pheasant. You will need to start preparing it about 30 minutes before the pheasant is cooked.*

Pollo ai Peperoni
Chicken with Bell Peppers

Serves 4
Preparation: about 1 hour
Cooking: approximately 45 minutes
Recipe grading: easy

- 4 tablespoons/2 oz/60 g butter
- 5 tablespoons extra-virgin olive oil
- ½ tablespoon finely chopped fresh rosemary leaves
- 1 roasting chicken, cut into 8 pieces
- 1 bay leaf
- 1¾ cups/14 fl oz/400 ml hot chicken stock (homemade or bouillon cube)
- 4 green or yellow bell peppers/capsicums
- 6–7 anchovy fillets canned in oil, finely chopped
- 2 cloves garlic, peeled and slightly crushed
- salt to taste
- freshly ground black pepper
- 4 tablespoons wine vinegar

Suggested wine: a dry white (Roero Arneis)

Place half the butter and 1 tablespoon of the oil in a large nonstick skillet (frying pan) over a moderate heat. Add the rosemary and, after 30 seconds, the pieces of chicken and the bay leaf. ⮞ Increase the heat slightly and fry the chicken pieces for 6–8 minutes, turning them frequently to brown evenly. ⮞ Add just over half the stock and cover. Cook for about 25 minutes or until done, adding more hot stock as necessary. ⮞ While the chicken is cooking, slice the bell peppers lengthwise in half, then remove the stalk, seeds, and pulpy inner core. Cut into ¾ in/2 cm wide strips. ⮞ Melt the remaining butter in a saucepan. Stir in the anchovies, crushing them so that they dissolve into the butter. ⮞ Add the strips of pepper and the garlic. Season with a little salt and pepper. ⮞ Simmer over a moderate heat for 15 minutes, gradually drizzling in the vinegar. ⮞ Remove the garlic and the bay leaf and discard. ⮞ Add the bell pepper mixture to the chicken. Simmer for 10 minutes more, stirring and turning now and then. ⮞ Serve hot.

Caponet

Stuffed Zucchini Flowers

Serves 4
Preparation: 30 minutes
Cooking: 5 minutes
Recipe grading: fairly easy

Place the cooked meat, sausage meat, garlic, parsley, eggs, and parmesan in a mixing bowl and combine thoroughly until smooth and well mixed. ❧ Alternatively, place the cooked meat, sausage meat, garlic, and parsley in a food processor. Add the eggs and parmesan and process. ❧ Taste for salt and pepper and season if required. ❧ Handling the zucchini flowers gently, remove the pistils and stamens from the middle of each flower and remove any tiny insects. ❧ Rinse gently if required, although they will stay firmer if left dry. ❧ Use a teaspoon to stuff the flowers, leaving enough room to delicately pinch and twist the petal tips together to enclose the filling. ❧ Heat the butter in a large nonstick skillet (frying pan) until it has stopped foaming. Add the stuffed flowers and fry over a moderate heat until they are pale golden brown all over. ❧ Remove the flowers from the skillet. Drain briefly on paper towels, and serve at once.

- 1¾ cups/7 oz/200 g very finely chopped boiled or roast meat
- 4 oz/125 g cooked pork sausage meat, finely chopped
- 1 large clove garlic, finely chopped
- 1 tablespoon finely chopped parsley
- 2 eggs
- 2–3 tablespoons freshly grated parmesan cheese
- 20 very fresh zucchini/courgette flowers
- about 6 tablespoons/3 oz/90 g butter

Suggested wine: a light, dry white
(Cortese dell'Alto Monferrato)

This dish is a specialty of the Alba province. Unless you grow zucchini (courgettes) yourself it can be difficult to get hold of fresh, firm flowers. Look for them in the stores and markets in early summer.

Verdure

Garlic is one of the most widely used vegetables in Piedmontese cooking. Cooks in this region are not afraid of the strong, pungent taste and odor and they use it freely to flavor a wide variety of dishes. Other commonly used vegetables include bell peppers (celebrated with a special summer festival at Carmagnola, near Turin), asparagus, artichokes, cardoons (close relatives of artichokes), onions, tomatoes, sugar peas, beans, and spinach. In traditional cuisine vegetables were served as side dishes or appetizers; nowadays, as modern lifestyles encourage people toward lighter diets, vegetable dishes have been rediscovered, and are coming into their own as healthy alternatives to meat-based meals.

Asparagi alla Piemontese

Asparagus Piedmont-Style

Serves 4
Preparation: 5 minutes
Cooking: about 20 minutes
Recipe grading: easy

Trim the tough lower parts off the asparagus, leaving only the tender top part. ❧ Rinse the stalks carefully to avoid damaging them and steam for about 10 minutes. They should be tender but still firm. ❧ Melt the butter in a large nonstick skillet (frying pan). Spread out the asparagus in it with the tips all facing the same way. ❧ Season lightly with salt and pepper. Cook in the butter for 6–7 minutes: shaking the pan gently backward and forward to turn them so that they finish cooking evenly. ❧ Place a layer of fontina slices over the asparagus. Cover the skillet and cook for 2–3 minutes more, or until the cheese has melted. ❧ Serve at once.

- 3½ lb/1.5 kg medium green asparagus stalks
- 4 tablespoons/2 oz/60 g butter
- salt to taste
- freshly ground white pepper
- 4 oz/125 g fontina cheese, very thinly sliced

Suggested wine: a dry, fruity white (Roero Arneis)

The asparagus grown on the Monferrato limestone massif in Piedmont is renowned for the fullness and subtlety of its flavor.

Carciofi in Fricassea

Artichokes with Egg and Lemon Sauce

Serves 4

Preparation: 10 minutes

Cooking: 20–25 minutes

Recipe grading: easy

- 8 very young globe artichokes
- 2–3 tablespoons lemon juice
- 4 tablespoons/2 oz/60 g butter
- salt to taste
- 3 egg yolks
- 2 tablespoons light/single cream
- 3–4 tablespoons cold water
- 1 tablespoon finely chopped parsley (optional)
- freshly ground white pepper

Suggested wine: a young, dry white (Monferrato Bianco Vivace)

Cut off the stalks and remove the lower, outermost leaves of the artichokes. Use kitchen scissors to snip off the top quarter from each of the remaining leaves. ❧ Preparing one artichoke at a time, slice into quarters from top to bottom and, unless they are tiny artichoke buds, remove the hairy "choke" from the center. ❧ Cut each quarter into 2–3 thin slices, dropping them immediately into a large bowl of cold water acidulated with 1 tablespoon of lemon juice to prevent discoloration. ❧ Melt the butter in a skillet (frying pan) and add the well-drained artichoke slices. Sprinkle with a little salt and cook over a moderate heat. ❧ Stir and turn frequently, adding 1–2 tablespoons of hot water at intervals to keep them moist. They will probably take about 20 minutes to cook. Test to make sure they are tender. ❧ Beat the egg yolks, cream, and cold water lightly together in a small bowl with the parsley (if using), salt, and pepper. ❧ Sprinkle the remaining lemon juice over the cooked artichokes and reduce the heat to very low. ❧ Pour the egg mixture over the artichokes and stir. The egg mixture should turn creamy and thicken somewhat (this will only take about 2 minutes; do not allow the eggs to scramble). ❧ Serve at once.

Piedmontese artichokes are just one of the many outstandingly high-quality vegetables grown in plentiful supply in this region.

Asparagi allo Zabaione

Asparagus with Sabayon Sauce

Serves 4
Preparation: 15 minutes
Cooking: about 25 minutes
Recipe grading: fairly easy

- 3½ lb/1.5 kg medium green asparagus stalks
- 4 egg yolks
- 8 tablespoons dry white wine
- 2 tablespoons/1 oz/30 g butter, at room temperature
- salt to taste

Suggested wine: a light, dry white (Langhe Arneis)

Trim off the tough lower parts of the asparagus stalks, leaving only 1½ in/4 cm of the paler section attached to the tips. Use a sharp knife to scrape off any remaining dirt. Rinse well under cold running water. ❧ Steam the asparagus until the stalks are tender but not mushy. The cooking time will vary depending on the freshness and thickness of the asparagus. ❧ While the asparagus is cooking, use the egg yolks, wine, butter, and salt to make the Sabayon sauce, following the method given on page 103 for sweet Zabaglione sauce. ❧ Pour the sauce over the asparagus tips and serve very hot.

Taccole alla Panna

Sugar Peas with Cream

Serves 4
Preparation: 5 minutes
Cooking: 8–10 minutes
Recipe grading: easy

Rinse the sugar peas and string them if necessary. ❧ Place in a saucepan of boiling salted water and cook for 8–10 minutes, or until tender. ❧ When they have about 2 minutes cooking time left, heat the butter in a small saucepan until it turns golden brown. ❧ Drain the sugar peas and place in a heated serving dish. Cover quickly with the cream. Sprinkle with the grated parmesan. Pour the very hot butter over the top. Serve at once.

- 1 lb/500 g sugar peas/snow peas/ mange-tout
- salt to taste
- 4 tablespoons/2 oz/60 g butter
- 6 tablespoons heavy/double cream
- ½ cup/2 oz/60 g freshly grated parmesan cheese

Suggested wine: a dry rosé (Mosaico)

These tender little peas, also called snow peas or mange-tout, are eaten whole, pods and all. If you can't find them, substitute fresh young ordinary peas in their pods.

Cipolle Ripiene

Stuffed Onions

Peel the onions and boil for 10–15 minutes in salted water. ❧ Drain and set aside to cool a little. ❧ Cut the onions in half horizontally and scoop out enough flesh from their centers to form a hollow into which half an egg would fit. ❧ Finely chop the flesh you have removed. ❧ Break up the sausage meat (from a skinned fresh spicy sausage) and mix it with the ground meat. Cook this mixture in half the butter in a skillet (frying pan) for 6–7 minutes, then transfer to a mixing bowl. ❧ Add the chopped onion, parmesan, egg, peach brandy, and salt and pepper to taste. Combine very thoroughly. ❧ Use this stuffing to fill the hollowed half onions, heaping it up into a smooth mound. ❧ Arrange the onions close together in a single layer in a roasting pan or dish greased with butter. ❧ Sprinkle with the breadcrumbs and place a sliver of butter on each one. ❧ Pour 3–4 tablespoons hot stock or water into the the bottom of the dish. ❧ Bake the onions in a preheated oven at 350°F/180°C/gas 4 for 40–45 minutes, adding a little more stock or water to stop them sticking if necessary. ❧ Serve hot or at room temperature.

Serves 4
Preparation: 30 minutes
Cooking: about 1 hour
Recipe grading: easy

- 6 medium Spanish onions
- 2 oz/60 g meat from a fresh Italian sausage
- 1³/₄ cups/7 oz/200 g ground veal or beef
- 5 tablespoons/2¹/₂ oz/70 g butter
- ³/₄ cup/3 oz/90 g freshly grated parmesan cheese
- 1 large egg
- 1 tablespoon peach brandy
- salt to taste
- freshly ground white pepper
- 3 tablespoons fine dry breadcrumbs
- a little hot stock (homemade or bouillon cube) or water

Suggested wine: a medium or dry, lightly sparkling red (Barbera del Monferrato Frizzante or Barbera del Monferrato Vivace)

. *For a sweeter dish, add a finely crumbled amaretto cookie to the stuffing mixture.*

Spinaci alla Piemontese

Spinach Piedmont-Style

Serves 4
Preparation: 10 minutes
Cooking: 8–10 minutes
Recipe grading: easy

- 2 lb/1 kg fresh spinach leaves
- 4 tablespoons/2 oz/60 g butter
- 2 anchovy fillets, crumbled
- ½ clove garlic, finely chopped
- salt to taste
- freshly ground white pepper
- slices of bread fried in olive oil

Suggested wine: a light, dry white
(Cortese di Gavi)

Wash the spinach thoroughly and cook for 2–3 minutes in a covered saucepan. ☙ Leave to cool a little, then squeeze out as much moisture as possible. Chop coarsely. ☙ Melt the butter in a saucepan, then add the anchovies and the garlic. Crush the anchovies into the butter with the back of a wooden spoon so that they dissolve as they cook gently. ☙ Add the spinach and season with salt and pepper to taste. ☙ Cook for 6–7 minutes over a fairly low heat, stirring frequently. ☙ Transfer to a preheated serving dish and surround with the slices of fried bread.

Crisply fried bread makes the ideal foil for the subtle anchovy and garlic flavoring of the spinach.

Taccole in Salsa del Povr'om

Sugar Peas in Poor Man's Sauce

Serves 4
Preparation: 10 minutes
Cooking: 10 minutes
Recipe grading: easy

Prepare the Poor Man's Sauce. ❧ Rinse the sugar peas and boil in salted water for 10 minutes. ❧ Drain the sugar peas and arrange on a preheated serving platter. ❧ Cover with the Poor Man's Sauce and serve immediately.

- 1 quantity Poor Man's Sauce (see recipe, page 18)
- 1 lb/500 g sugar peas/snow peas/ mange-tout

Suggested wine: a young, dry, lightly sparkling white (Cortese di Gavi Frizzante)

Pomodori alla Novarese

Tomatoes Novara-Style

Serves 4
Preparation: 30 minutes
Cooking: about 1 hour
Recipe grading: easy

- 8 medium tomatoes
- 2 eggs
- fine, dry breadcrumbs
- 3 tablespoons/1½ oz/45 g butter

FOR THE FILLING:

- 1 tablespoon very finely chopped onion
- 2 tablespoons/1 oz/30 g butter
- scant 1 cup/6 oz/180 g Italian Arborio rice
- 1 cup/8 fl oz/250ml boiling stock (homemade or bouillon cube)
- ½ cup/2 oz/60 g freshly grated parmesan cheese
- salt to taste
- freshly ground black pepper

Suggested wine: a dry red
(Grignolino d'Asti)

Rinse and dry the tomatoes and cut a slice ½ in/1 cm thick off the stalk end. Set these little "lids" aside. ❧ Scoop out and discard the seeds and the central fleshy parts which divide the seed chambers. ❧ To make the filling, fry the onion in the butter over a low heat until the onion is transparent but not brown. ❧ Add the rice and cook for 2–3 minutes, stirring continuously. ❧ Pour in about half the stock and stir continuously over a moderate heat until the liquid has been absorbed. ❧ Continue to add a little more stock at intervals, stirring and cooking until the rice is tender but still fairly firm to the bite. This will take about 10–15 minutes. ❧ The risotto should be less moist than usual. When it is ready, turn off the heat and stir in the parmesan. Season to taste with salt and pepper. ❧ Stuff the tomatoes with the risotto and cover each one neatly with its lid. ❧ Beat the eggs lightly in a bowl and then carefully dip the stuffed tomatoes into the egg. Coat with the breadcrumbs. ❧ Use a little butter to grease a fairly shallow ovenproof dish into which the tomatoes will fit snugly. Place them in a single layer, lid-side uppermost, and top each one with a flake of butter. ❧ Bake in a preheated oven at 400°F/200°C/gas 6 for 25–30 minutes. ❧ Serve hot or at room temperature.

When preparing a simple risotto or even plain boiled rice, make a double quantity and use half to fill the tomatoes. This dish can be prepared a day in advance.

Fagiolata
Bean Casserole

Place the beans, pork rind, and onion in a fireproof earthenware casserole or heavy-bottomed saucepan with just enough cold water to cover them. ❧ Bring to a boil over a high heat, then simmer gently over a much lower heat for 1½ hours, stirring now and then. ❧ The liquid should reduce considerably, but the beans should remain very moist. Add a little more boiling water if necessary. ❧ Add the tomato paste, oil, rosemary, and cloves, and season with salt and pepper to taste. Continue cooking for 30 more minutes over a low heat. ❧ Serve hot.

Serves 4
Preparation: 15 minutes
Cooking: about 2 hours
Recipe grading: easy

- 1–1½ lb/500–750 g fresh borlotti beans, net shelled weight
- about 12 oz/350 g fresh pork rind, cut into 1 in/2.5 cm squares
- 1 large onion, peeled and sliced
- 1–2 tablespoons tomato paste
- 4–5 tablespoons extra virgin olive oil
- scant 1 tablespoon chopped fresh rosemary leaves
- 2 cloves
- salt to taste
- freshly ground black pepper

Suggested wine: a dry red (Nebbiolo)

Originally a peasant dish for winter, this recipe is also popular with today's more prosperous Piedmontese. Bean casserole is often served with polenta (see recipe, page 58) and cotechino sausage (see method for cooking cotechino sausage on page 64). For a slightly different dish, add sliced savoy cabbage to the beans about 30 minutes before they are cooked. If you can't get fresh borlotti beans, use 1½ cups/10 oz/300 g of dried borlotti beans soaked in cold water for 8–10 hours.

Dolci

Unlike many other regions of Italy, Piedmont and the Val d'Aosta boast an almost infinite variety of desserts, cakes, cookies, chocolates, and candies of every imaginable kind. The woodlands provide fresh hazelnuts and chestnuts each fall which are imaginatively combined with sugars, spices, and various local and imported products to make a mouthwatering array of candies. From the simplest of cooked creams and custards to the rich depths of *Torta Gianduia* (Piedmontese Chocolate Cake) and *Coppa Torino* (Sweet Chestnut Trifle), there is something for all tastes and every occasion. To round things off, the regional capital, Turin, is the home of the very best in Italian chocolate-making, while many of the smaller towns have long-standing traditions of cookie-making.

Ciliege al Barolo

Cherries in Red Wine

Place the cherries, sugar, wine, cinnamon, and orange strips together in a saucepan. Cook gently, uncovered, over a low heat for 25–30 minutes. Stir very carefully from time to time so as not to damage the cherries. ❧ Use a slotted spoon to take the cherries out of the liquid, letting them drain briefly as you do so, and transfer them to a serving dish. ❧ Remove and discard the cinnamon. ❧ Add the red currant jelly to the cooking liquid and reduce over a moderate heat. Then pour over the cherries. ❧ The cherries can be eaten while still warm, but they are better served cold with generous spoonfuls of freshly whipped cream.

Serves 4
Preparation: 10 minutes
Cooking: about 30 minutes
Recipe grading: easy

- 1½ lb/750 g pitted cherries
- about 1 cup/8 oz/250 g sugar
- 2 cups/16 fl oz/500 ml full-bodied, dry red wine (preferably Barolo)
- a 1¼ in/3 cm piece of cinnamon stick
- 2–3 pieces of orange zest/rind, cut into very thin, short strips
- 2 tablespoons red currant jelly

Suggested wine: a sweet, lightly sparkling red (Brachetto d'Acqui)

Wine plays a very important part in the cooking of Piedmont and, when partnered with fruit, forms a happy marriage. Most recipes call for Barolo, but other good-quality red wines are also suitable.

Mont Blanc

Marrons Glacés with Rum and Cream

Serves 4

Preparation: 15 minutes +
  20–30 minutes' soaking

Recipe grading: easy

- 14 oz/400 g pieces of marrons glacés/candied chestnuts
- 6 tablespoons rum
- 1½ cups/12 fl oz/350 ml unsweetened whipped cream

Suggested wine: a medium sweet, light
  young red (Malvasia di Castelnuovo
  Don Bosco Frizzante)

Place the pieces of marrons glacés in a bowl. Sprinkle them with the rum and leave to soak for 20–30 minutes. ✎ Put the rum-soaked pieces of marrons glacés through a food mill with the large-gauge slotted disk fitted. Then process them again through the food mill, this time with the medium gauge disk. They will form little spaghetti-like shapes. ✎ Let the processed marrons glacés fall into the center of the serving dish as they come out of the food mill, so that they form a dome-shaped mound. ✎ Cover the mound carefully with the whipped cream, smoothing the surface, or leaving it uneven, as preferred. ✎ Serve at room temperature or chill for 2 hours before serving.

For a very impressive and professional finishing touch, decorate the dessert with caramel threads. Place scant ⅓ cup/2½ oz/75 g superfine (caster) sugar in a small saucepan with scant 1 tablespoon water and 8–10 drops of lemon juice. Stir over a moderate heat until the sugar melts and caramelizes to a deep golden color. ✎ Remove from the heat and, taking a tablespoonful at a time, let the caramel fall in thin threads so that it winds its way around the chestnut mound in a spiral. It does not matter if this is not very symmetrical; let a few threads come vertically up the sides of the "mountain" and you will have enclosed it in a golden cage of caramel. ✎ Serve the whipped cream separately.

The original recipe involves shelling and cooking the sweet chestnuts, removing their thin skins, and so on, a dauntingly laborious process. This much shorter method gives equally good results. Broken pieces of marrons glacés/candied chestnuts are readily available in good delicatessens and larger supermarkets.

Serves 4

Preparation: 5–10 minutes + 2 hours'
  chilling

Cooking: 8–10 minutes

Recipe grading: easy

Panna Cotta
Cooked Cream

- 2 cups/16 fl oz/500 ml heavy/double cream
- ²∕₃ cup/5 fl oz/150 ml whole/full cream milk
- ¹∕₃ cup/3 oz/90 g superfine/caster sugar
- 2 teaspoons vanilla extract/essence
- 2–3 tablespoons peach brandy
- 1 heaped tablespoon unflavored gelatin powder
- 3¹∕₂ tablespoons cold water

Suggested wine: a sweet white
  (Moscato d'Asti)

For a slightly different flavor, replace the peach brandy with the same quantity of rum or very strong black coffee, or replace the vanilla with a generous dash of ground cinnamon. In Italy, each little Panna Cotta *is often served with 1 tablespoon of mixed berry compote diluted with a little water.*

Heat the cream, milk, sugar, vanilla extract, and peach brandy in a saucepan over a moderate heat to just below boiling point. ❧ Meanwhile, sprinkle the gelatin onto the cold water in a bowl and leave to stand for 3 minutes (without stirring) to soften. ❧ Remove the saucepan from the heat and beat in the gelatin with a balloon whisk until it has completely dissolved. ❧ Pour the creamy mixture into little molds or individual glass dishes and set aside to cool. ❧ Refrigerate for at least 2 hours before serving.

Zabaione

Zabaglione

Beat the egg yolks and sugar together in a bowl with a balloon whisk or electric beater until they are fluffy, smooth, and almost white. ❧ Gradually add the Marsala wine while beating vigorously. ❧ Place the bowl over a saucepan half full of simmering water (making sure that the bowl does not touch the water) and continue beating. After a few minutes the egg mixture will start to thicken and will rise up in the bowl. When the whisk or beater is lifted above it, there will be an unbroken "ribbon" of mixture. This means the zabaglione is done. Remove it from the heat at once and transfer to little dishes or stemmed glasses. It can be served hot with cookies, or cold, possibly with mixed berry fruit. ❧ If left to cool completely, this quantity of zabaglione can then be folded into 1 cup/8 fl oz/250 ml unsweetened whipped cream. Spoon into little glass dishes and chill in the refrigerator for at least 1 hour. The resulting mousse is good with poached pears or sprinkled with coarsely chopped walnuts.

Serves 4
Preparation: 6–8 minutes
Cooking: 4–6 minutes
Recipe grading: fairly easy

- 4 egg yolks
- 8 tablespoons superfine/caster sugar
- 8 tablespoons dry Marsala wine

Suggested wine: a sweet dessert white (Moscadile)

The old-fashioned way of measuring the sugar and the Marsala was to stipulate a certain number of "half eggshells full." This might seem quaint nowadays but the aim was to ensure that proportions were correct, no matter what size the eggs. Zabaglione can be used as a filling for cakes and as a sauce for puddings, and also makes the basis for an excellent ice cream.

Chocolate, Cookies and Desserts

The huge variety of cookies, cakes, desserts, and chocolates in Piedmontese cuisine is due in large part to the chefs of the Dukes of Savoy, who delighted in inventing ever new and delicious sweets to tempt the palates of their aristocratic masters. Zabaglione is said to have been invented by the personal cook of Charles Emanuele I, Duke of Savoy. The exquisite combination of egg, sweet Marsala wine, sugar, and cinnamon were meant to sustain and reinvigorate the delicate Duke. The distinctive curved shape of krumiri cookies (left), known throughout Piedmont under different names, is said to have been created to imitate the curves of King Vittorio Emanuele's mustaches! Amaretti cookies were invented by yet another Savoyan chef, Francesco Moriondo, who first mixed almonds, sugar, and egg whites in 1750 to bake these delicious little treats.

APRICOT POCKETS

1 cup/8 fl oz/250 ml white wine

6 tablespoons/2 oz/60 g brown sugar

2 tablespoons honey

1 teaspoon cinnamon

12 apricots

10 crushed amaretti cookies/macaroons

2 tablespoons each of pine nuts and raisins

Cook the wine, brown sugar, honey and cinnamon in a saucepan over a high heat until syrupy. ❧ Cut out 6 pieces of nonstick baking paper to make the "pockets." Place 2 pitted, halved apricots in each pocket, pour a little of the syrup over them, sprinkle with the crumbled amaretti and decorate with the pine nuts and raisins. ❧ Tie up the pockets with kitchen string and bake in a preheated 400°F/ 200°C/ gas 6 oven for about 15 minutes. Serve hot or warm.

According to an old saying "Necessity is the mother of invention", and this is certainly the case with the celebrated Gianduiotto chocolate. When stocks of cocoa dwindled during the Napoleonic Wars, sweetmakers in Turin decided to add finely ground hazelnuts to their scarce supplies of cocoa. The first gianduiotto in history duely appeared in 1865 and was named after a mask used in traditional Piedmontese theater. Today these mouthwatering chocolates are exported all over the world.

Nutella, a mouthwatering mixture of chocolate and hazelnut, is another Piedmontese invention whose fame has spread throughout the world.

CHOCOLATE TRUFFLES

Makes thirty truffles

4 tablespoons/2.oz/60 g butter
2$^1\!/_2$ oz/75 g confectioners'/icing sugar
2 egg yolks
$^1\!/_2$ cup/3$^1\!/_2$ fl oz/100 ml light/single cream
6 drops vanilla extract/essence
12 squares/12 oz/300 g semi-sweet chocolate, grated
4 tablespoons cocoa powder

Cream the butter and confectioners' sugar, then beat in the egg yolks one at a time. ✄ Bring the cream to a boil over a moderate heat, then stir in the vanilla extract. Pour the boiling cream into the butter mixture, then stir in the chocolate. Set aside in the refrigerator for at least two hours. ✄ Using a tablespoon, form into balls and roll in the cocoa powder. ✄ Store in the refrigerator until it is time to serve.

Serves 6

Preparation: 30 minutes + 1 hour's chilling for the pastry

Cooking: 40 minutes

Recipe grading: fairly easy

FOR THE FILLING:

• 2 lb/1 kg firm cooking pears

• 4½ tablespoons/2½ oz/75 g sugar

• 1¼ cups/10 fl oz/300 ml very good-quality dry red wine

• dash of ground cinnamon

• 2 tablespoons unsweetened cocoa powder

• 10 amaretti cookies, coarsely crushed

FOR THE SWEET PASTRY:

• 2 cups/8 oz/250 g all-purpose/plain flour

• scant 1 cup/3½ oz/100 g very fine yellow cornmeal

• ½ cup/4 oz/125 g superfine/caster sugar

• dash of salt

• ⅔ cup/5 oz/150 g butter, at room temperature, cut in tiny flakes or slivers

• 3 egg yolks

Suggested wine: a sweet white (Moscato di Strevi Banfi)

The "Martin sech" or "Martine" variety of locally grown little pears are traditionally used for this dessert, but any firm-fleshed cooking pear is suitable.

Crostata di Pere
Pear Pie

Peel the pears. Cut lengthwise into quarters, and core. Then cut each quarter lengthwise into 3 slices. ❧ Place the slices of pear in a saucepan in which they will just fit comfortably. Add the sugar, wine, and cinnamon, and cook gently over a moderate heat for 10 minutes. ❧ Pour off the cooking liquid, then sprinkle the pears with the cocoa. Set aside to cool. ❧ To make the pastry, begin by mixing the two types of flour thoroughly in a bowl. Stir in the sugar and salt. ❧ Using a fork, stir in the butter, followed by the egg yolks. Work the ingredients quickly together to form a mixture which resembles fine breadcrumbs. Gather these together by hand and combine (do not knead) to form a soft ball of pastry dough which is not in the least elastic. ❧ Use two-thirds of the pastry to line the bottom and sides of an ungreased 8½ in/22 cm diameter flan or pie pan (at least 1½ in/4 cm deep). Do this by placing the pastry in the pie pan and gradually working it into a lining of even thickness using your fingertips. ❧ Chill the uncooked pie shell (flan case) in the refrigerator for 1 hour. ❧ Wrap the remaining pastry dough in plastic wrap (cling film) and put it a cool place, preferably not in the refrigerator as it still has to be rolled out. ❧ Take the pie shell out of the refrigerator. Sprinkle evenly with the crumbled amaretti cookies and arrange the pears on top. ❧ Roll out the remaining pastry dough into a round slightly larger than the diameter of the pie pan. Place this on top of the pears, pinching the pastry edges together to seal. Pierce a few little holes in the pie lid with a fine skewer. ❧ Bake in a preheated oven at 400°F/200°C/gas 6 for about 40 minutes. ❧ Let cool slightly in the pan before transferring to a serving plate. Leave to cool completely before serving.

Serves 4–6

Preparation: 20 minutes

Cooking: 1 hour

Recipe grading: fairly easy

- 1 cup/8 oz/250 g sugar
- ½ teaspoon lemon juice
- 2 tablespoons cold water
- 3½ cups/1½ pints/800 ml whole/ full cream milk
- 6 eggs
- 2–3 tablespoons unsweetened cocoa powder
- 2 oz/60 g amaretti cookies, finely pounded
- 3 tablespoons rum

Suggested wine: a sweet dessert white (Malvasia di Nus)

Bonet

Piedmontese Chocolate Egg Custard

Place half of the sugar in a small saucepan with the lemon juice and water and place over a moderate heat. ❧ As soon as the sugar caramelizes to golden brown, pour it into a warmed 9 cup/3½ pint/2 liter (or slightly smaller) ring tube mold. Tip the mold to coat the inside evenly before the caramel hardens. Set aside. ❧ Heat the milk gently until just tepid. ❧ Use a balloon whisk or electric beater to beat the eggs very thoroughly in a bowl with the remaining sugar. Add the cocoa powder carefully and mix well. ❧ Stir in the warm milk, followed by the amaretti cookies and rum. ❧ Pour this mixture into the caramel-lined mold. cover the mold with a piece of foil and place in a larger ovenproof container half filled with cold water. Cook in a preheated oven at 300°F/150°C/gas 2 for 1 hour, or until set. ❧ Take the mold out of the oven and leave to cool for 15–20 minutes before unmolding carefully onto a dish. ❧ Serve at room temperature or chill for a few hours in the refrigerator before serving, as preferred.

In an unusual and interesting version of this recipe, the rum is replaced by a slightly smaller quantity of Fernet Branca liquer, and 2–3 tablespoons of strong black coffee are added.

Pere al Barolo

Pears in Red Wine

Serves 4
Preparation: 10 minutes
Cooking: about 1 hour
Recipe grading: easy

- 8 small Martin sech or Martine pears, or 4 large, firm cooking pears
- 1 cup/8 oz/250 g sugar
- 3½ cups/1½ pints/500 ml full-bodied, dry red wine (preferably Barolo)
- 3 cloves
- 2 pieces of lemon peel
- ¾ in/2 cm piece of cinnamon (optional)

Suggested wine: a sweet aromatic rosé (Malvasia di Casorzo d'Asti Rosato)

The traditional variety of small, rust-colored pear ("Martin sech" or "Martine") used for this recipe is now increasingly difficult to find and may soon disappear altogether. Other firm-flesh cooking pears can be used in its place.

Peel the pears carefully, leaving them whole with the stalk still attached. ❧ Transfer to a deep, fireproof casserole into which they fit snugly, standing upright, stalks uppermost. Sprinkle with half the sugar; then pour in the wine, and add the cloves, lemon peel and, if liked, the cinnamon. ❧ Place in a preheated oven at 350°F/180°C/gas 4 and cook for about 1 hour, or until tender. The time will vary depending on how firm the pears are: test by inserting a thin skewer deep into one to see if it is tender. By this time they should be an attractive russet color. ❧ Lift the pears carefully out of the wine and place upright in a serving dish or, better still, in individual glass dishes. ❧ Reduce the cooking liquid over a moderate heat until it has thickened to a pouring syrup. Discard the cloves, lemon peel, and cinnamon and pour the syrup over the pears. ❧ Serve at room temperature.

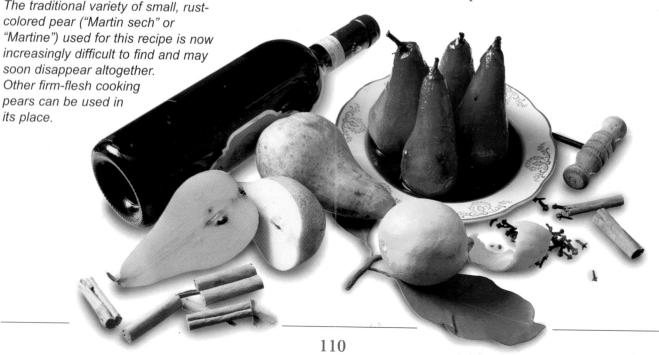

Pesche Ripiene

Stuffed Peaches

Serves 4
Preparation: 20–25 minutes
Cooking: 35–40 minutes
Recipe grading: easy

Rinse and dry the peaches, then cut them in half. Remove the pits and reserve. ❧ Use a melon baller or metal spoon to scoop out the hollows leaving a "wall" of about ¼ in/5 mm. Use a fork to crush the flesh in a fairly large bowl. ❧ Place half the sugar in a food processor with the almonds and grind. ❧ Mix the almonds and sugar into the crushed peach flesh in a bowl. Add the cocoa powder, egg, and amaretti and mix thoroughly, moistening with enough wine to make a soft paste that will hold its shape. ❧ Fill each peach half with this mixture, heaping it up to form a smoothly rounded mound. ❧ Use some of the butter to grease a shallow ovenproof dish just large enough to accommodate the peach halves in one layer, then transfer them to it. ❧ Crack open the peach pits and take out the kernels. Select the plumpest, soundest kernels and blanch them in boiling water for 1 minute. Peel off the thin skin, and separate the two halves of each kernel. Place half in the center of each stuffed peach. ❧ Cover with a flake of butter and sprinkle with the remaining sugar. ❧ Pour the rest of the wine into the dish and bake in a preheated oven at 350°F/180°C/gas 4 for 35–40 minutes.

- 4 large ripe yellow peaches
- generous ⅓ cup/3½ oz/100 g superfine/caster sugar
- 2 tablespoons shelled almonds
- 1 tablespoon unsweetened cocoa powder
- 1 egg
- 10 amaretti cookies, finely pounded
- 1¼ cups/10 fl oz/300 ml Moscato (Muscat) white dessert wine
- 2½ tablespoons/1½ oz/45 g butter

Suggested wine: a sweet dessert white (Malvasia di Nus)

The unmistakable flavor of the amaretti cookies gives this typically Piedmontese dessert a very distinctive taste. Delicious warm, these peaches are also very good when they have cooled to room temperature.

Piedmontese Sparkling Wines

Piedmont reigns supreme in Italy for the variety and range of the sparkling wines it produces. Sweet, medium, or dry, there is something for everyone and for all occasions. Although Charles Albert, King of Piedmont and Sardinia, was the first to express the desire to drink "Italian champagne," it wasn't until almost fifty years after his death that the first bottle of Italian bubbly hit the market in 1895. Made from the white Moscato grape, Piedmontese sparkling

wine is made according to a special method, known as *charmat*, which is a way of fermenting the wine in tanks, or even single bottles, to attain that fine balance of fragrance and sparkle for which the wines are famous. It is much cheaper than the *champenoise* method used in France to make champagne. Production of Italian sparkling wines has soared in recent years as both local and international demand for these light joyful wines has increased.

Asti spumante is not aged. The wired down cork can be popped just a few months after the autumn harvest. It can be served in either wide-brimmed glasses which exalt its intense aroma, or in narrow flutes which conserve its sparkle for as long as possible. It is good with all kinds of desserts and its low alcohol content makes it suitable for family occasions where even children can take a sip. The year of production is rarely given on the label, so be sure to buy from reliable retailers who can garantee the wine's freshness.

The normal process for making Asti spumante involves soft crushing of the grapes and settling the juice before filtering and transferring to storage tanks. The whole process only takes about six weeks from fermentation to bottling. Tanks of Asti are often chilled to near freezing to halt fermentation and held until just before the Christmas holidays when demand is at its peak. It is shipped as soon as possible after bottling to ensure its freshness for the buyer.

There are numerous treasures of art and history in Piedmont. It is the ideal location for a peaceful "gastronomic journey" and, surprisingly, is still reasonably unspoiled by mass tourism. Casale Monferrato (bottom left, facing page) and Asti (above) are just two of the Piedmontese towns worth a visit.

Moscato d'Asti, a sweet dessert wine, is one of the oldest wines of Piedmont. According to local tradition, it has been made since Ancient Roman times. It is best when young, and should in any case be consumed within two years of production. Made from the white Moscato grape, it is produced mostly by small wineries around Asti, Alessandria, and Cuneo. Although quite rare outside Piedmont, there is also a dry version of Moscato d'Asti . Served cool, it makes an excellent aperitif.

Torta di Nocciole

Hazelnut Cake

Serves 4

Preparation: 25 minutes

Cooking: 35–40 minutes

Recipe grading: fairly easy

- 1¼ cups/5 oz/150 g all-purpose/plain flour
- 1¼ cups/5 oz/150 g potato starch/flour
- 2½ teapoons baking powder
- 7 oz/200 g shelled hazelnuts
- dash of salt
- 3 large eggs
- scant 1 cup/7 oz/200 g superfine/caster sugar
- ⅔ cup/5 oz/150 g butter, at room temperature
- 2–3 tablespoons rum
- extra butter for greasing the cake pan

Suggested wine: a sweet or dry, sparkling wine (Asti Spumante)

The superb hazelnuts used in Piedmont's desserts, cakes, and confectionery come from the clay-covered chalk hills south of Alba, known as the Langhe.

Sift the two types of flour and the baking powder together into a mixing bowl. ❧ Grind the hazelnuts or pound them finely, then add to the bowl with the salt. ❧ Beat the eggs with the sugar in a separate bowl with a balloon whisk or electric beater until the mixture is very pale and fluffy. ❧ Continue beating as you gradually add the softened butter, a very small piece at a time. ❧ Gradually add the mixed dry ingredients, beating them in 1 tablespoon at a time. ❧ Finally beat in the rum. ❧ Grease and lightly flour an 8½ in/22 cm diameter springform cake pan. ❧ Turn the cake mixture into it (do not smooth or level out). ❧ Bake in a preheated oven at 350°F/180°C/gas 4 for 35–40 minutes. ❧ Leave the cake to cool in the pan for 10 minutes after you have removed it from the oven, then turn it out. ❧ Serve at room temperature.

Torta Gianduia
Piedmontese Chocolate Cake

Beat the egg yolks and confectioner's sugar in a mixing bowl until light and frothy. ✎ Stir in the flour and cocoa powder and mix well. ✎ Fold in the egg whites, followed by the melted butter. ✎ Grease and lightly flour a 8½ in/22 cm diameter springform cake pan. ✎ Add the cake mixture and bake in a preheated oven at 350°F/180°C/gas 4 for 35–40 minutes. ✎ Remove from the oven and turn out onto a cake rack to cool. ✎ To prepare the cream, first beat the egg yolks with the sugar until light and frothy. ✎ Stir in the flour, butter, chocolate, and vanilla flavoring, then gradually add the milk. ✎ Place over low heat and stir continuously until the mixture is thick and creamy. The mixture must not boil. When thick, set aside to cool a little. ✎ When the cake is cool, cut in half horizontally and cover one half with half the chocolate cream. Place the other half on top and cover with the remaining chocolate cream. ✎ Sprinkle with the almonds and serve.

Serves 6
Preparation: 30 minutes
Cooking: 45 minutes
Recipe grading: complicated

- 4 eggs, separated, whites beaten to stiff peaks
- ¾ cup/5 oz/150 g confectioners'/icing sugar
- 1¼ cups/5 oz/150 g all-purpose/plain flour
- 5 tablespoons bitter cocoa powder
- 4 tablespoons/2 oz/60 g butter, melted

FOR THE CREAM
- 2 egg yolks
- ⅔ cup/5 oz/150 g superfine/caster sugar
- ½ cup/2 oz/60 g all-purpose/plain flour
- 7 tablespoons/3½ oz/100 g butter
- 3½ squares/3½ oz/100 g dark unsweetened chocolate, grated
- ¼ teaspoon vanilla extract/essence
- 2 cups/16 fl oz/500 ml milk
- 4 tablespoons toasted, shelled almonds

Suggested wine: a sweet, sparkling wine (Asti Spumante)

This delicious cake is not simple to make, but is well worth the effort. Serve with coffee or tea in the late afternoon or with sweet champagne at the end of a special dinner party or family celebration.

Coppa Torino
Sweet Chestnut Trifle

To prepare the confectioner's custard, place the egg yolks, sugar, flour, lemon peel, and salt in a small saucepan. Mix thoroughly with a wooden spoon until they are pale and creamy. ✌ Add the boiling milk in a very thin stream, while stirring continuously. Place over a very low heat and continue stirring until the custard thickens; this will take only a few minutes. Do not let it boil or it will curdle. ✌ Remove from the heat and leave to cool, stirring at intervals to prevent a skin forming. If preparing the custard well in advance, cover with a piece of plastic wrap (cling film), resting it on the surface of the custard. ✌ Place a slice of sponge cake in the bottom of each glass or dish. Sprinkle with the rum diluted with 2–3 tablespoons of water. ✌ Cover with a ¾ in/2 cm thick layer of cool confectioner's custard. ✌ Sprinkle with the pieces of marrons glacés and top with whipped cream, drawn into peaks. ✌ Decorate each serving with a candied cherry and serve.

Serves 4
Preparation: 15 minutes
Cooking: 4–5 minutes
Recipe grading: easy

FOR THE CONFECTIONER'S CUSTARD:
- 2 egg yolks
- ½ cup/2 oz/60 g superfine/caster sugar
- ¼ cup/1 oz/30 g all-purpose/plain flour
- a little finely grated lemon peel
- dash of salt
- 1 cup/8 fl oz/250 ml boiling milk

- 4 slices sponge cake, ½ in/1 cm thick
- 6 tablespoons rum
- 4 heaped tablespoons broken pieces of marrons glacés/candied chestnuts
- 6 heaped tablespoons unsweetened whipped cream
- 4 candied/glacé cherries

Suggested wine: a dry, sparkling wine (Asti Spumante Brut)

This dessert was invented in Turin during the nineteenth century, but it has since been somewhat forgotten. Eye-catching and with an irresistible taste, it is well worth trying. It is traditionally assembled in champagne glasses, but little glass bowls or ice cream coupes can be used instead. To save time and trouble, buy the sponge cake. Buy pieces of marrons glacés, broken during preparation and cheaper than perfect marrons glacés/candied chestnuts.

Index

Acknowledgments

The Publishers would like to thank Mastrociliegia, Fiesole (Florence) who kindly lent props for photography.

All photos by MARCO LANZA except:

FARABOLAFOTO, MILAN: 6, 12, 24, 105TR, 117;
GIUSEPPE CARFAGNA, ROME: 2, 5, 7, 8, 9, 11T, 13, 20, 22B, 32B, 33, 48B, 49, 54, 72, 73, 74T, 97T, 112, 113 ARCHIVIO SCALA, FLORENCE: 78, 79T; OVERSEAS, MILAN 3, 11B, 32T, 55TL, 57T, 104T, 105TL;